D0561019

FAMILY FIRST

FAMILY FIRST

Winning the Parenting Game

DELORIS JORDAN

with Gregg Lewis

HarperSanFrancisco
An Imprint of HarperCollins*Publishers*

FAMILY FIRST: *Winning the Parenting Game.* Copyright © 1996 by Deloris Jordan. All rights reserved. Printed in the United States of America. No part of this book may be used or reproduced in any manner whatsoever without written permission except in the case of brief quotations embodied in critical articles and reviews. For information address HarperCollins Publishers, 10 East 53rd Street, New York, NY 10022.

HarperCollins Web Site: http://www.harpercollins.com
HarperCollins®, ■®, and HarperSanFrancisco™ are trademarks
of HarperCollins Publishers Inc.

FIRST EDITION

Library of Congress Cataloging-in-Publication Data

Jordan, Deloris.
    Family first : winning the parenting game / Deloris Jordan with
Gregg Lewis.
    ISBN 0–06–251388–5 (cloth)
    1. Parenting.   I. Lewis, Gregg A.   II. Title.
HQ755.8.J67   1996   96–10219
649'.1—dc20

98 99 00 ❖RRD(H) 10 9 8 7 6

To the memory of James Raymond Jordan

(who I usually called "Ray"),

A wonderful part of my life, all my adult life.

My partner in parenting.

A human being who, like all of us, made mistakes

But a husband who so enjoyed being a dad,

and was so committed to taking care of his family responsibilities

That we never had any doubt he truly loved us all.

We will forever love him for being the husband and father he was.

He will always be missed.

FAMILY FIRST

Wherever I go, whatever I'm doing, whomever I meet, I'm invariably introduced the same way: "This is Deloris Jordan—Michael's mom."

I always feel like interrupting (and sometimes I do) to say, "I'm also Ronald's mom, Delois's mom, Larry's mom, and Roslyn's mom." I have four other children I'm just as proud of and I love every bit as much as my world-famous son.

However, while I'm the mother of *five* wonderful and remarkable individuals, I realize that my identity as "Michael Jordan's mother" affords me many opportunities and responsibilities I wouldn't otherwise have. I know perfectly well that it's primarily because of the athletic accomplishments of my fourth child that I receive a constant stream of speaking invitations from organizations, schools, and churches around the country.

It's because Michael is often called the greatest basketball player in history that so many concerned mothers and fathers have asked me, "How can we encourage our son or daughter to pursue excellence?" Because countless articles and columns and books have been written about Michael's drive, determination, and strength of character, parents are always asking me, "What can we do to instill the kind of self-discipline and character our children will need to succeed in life?" And because my youngest son has become a role model recognized and emulated by millions (if not billions) of young people around the world, people often ask me, "Is there any way to protect my son or daughter from the dangers of peer pressure?"

But even more important than these questions of worried and desperate parents are the heart-rending needs of children that my role as "Michael's mom" has exposed me to. In 1989 Michael and I co-founded the Michael Jordan Foundation in order to better raise and channel funds to help disadvantaged children. Since then, the foundation has raised millions of dollars and distributed those funds to and through more than two dozen organizations doing remarkable work with children.

My volunteer role as foundation president has given me face-to-face exposure to the incredible suffering of many unforgettable children. It is their needs, combined with the questions and concerns parents share with me, that have convinced me families need encouragement and help today.

Just two quick stories to illustrate my point.

One of the regular features at our foundation's annual fund-raising gala is a celebrity auction where we sell donated items to the highest corporate or individual bidders. Each year since we began the auction, we've sold something we call "Bedtime Stories with Mrs. Jordan." For a bid that usually runs from $14,000 to $15,000, some generous individual or corporation can name a children's service agency that will then select ten to twenty disadvantaged children to participate in what must be one of the most unusual spend-the-night Christmas parties ever. Early one Saturday evening in December, just after closing time, the children and their chaperones arrive at the big F.A.O. Schwarz toy store on Michigan Avenue in downtown Chicago. Store officials unlock the doors to let the kids in and give them the run of the place for the evening. There's plenty of food, music, games, and everything else you'd ever expect to find at a Christmas party. But the dream-come-true fantasy for most of these wide-eyed kids is the chance to wander from one floor to another, opening and playing with any toy they choose in the whole huge store.

An hour or two before bedtime, I show up to meet the children and read them some of their favorite books, from a selection the store provides. When I finish reading, they play a little longer before climbing into sleeping bags rolled out right in the aisles of the store. As you might imagine, Sunday morning dawns very early; yet there never seem to be enough hours to play with everything before breakfast is served and the time comes for the party to end.

It's an unforgettable, once-in-a-lifetime experience for the kids who come. For me, it's an annual tradition that I look forward to all year long.

A couple years ago I arrived at F.A.O. Schwarz after the party was in full swing. Children had already scattered from one end of the store to the other—some sitting quietly on the floor dressing dolls almost as big as they were, others operating the network of electric trains speeding round and round a spectacular model train display, and a few squealing in delight while racing up and down the aisles in pursuit of (or being pursued by) some remote-controlled vehicle.

I spent my first hour or so at the party just wandering around, observing the joy of those children, and talking to them individually for a few minutes. Before I introduced myself to each youngster, one of the chaperones would give me a quick summary of that child's background.

As we approached a darling little eight- or nine-year-old girl sitting quietly on the floor by herself playing with a little doll baby, the chaperone pulled me aside to whisper, "We don't know much about Lisa [not her real name] yet. She's been at our group home for only two days. The police found her on Thursday, cold and hungry. She and her mother were living on a street corner, with little more than the clothes on their backs to shelter them from the wind on a cold December night in Chicago. Her mom's a drug addict and probably a prostitute. The girl's suffered terrible neglect for most, if not all, of her life. We suspect she's been abused. She's shy and naturally a little scared by all that's happened to her over the past forty-eight hours. She keeps asking about her mother."

I walked over and sat on the floor next to that precious little girl. "My name is Mrs. Jordan," I said. "What's yours?"

"Lisa," she answered softly. When she smiled shyly and looked up with those big brown eyes, I felt as if my heart would break. When I asked to see the doll she was playing with, Lisa showed me how to feed it so that the doll would immediately wet its pants. We both laughed at that. We played and talked a few minutes until I decided it was time to move on and meet some of the other children.

As I announced my intentions and stood, Lisa stood with me. And before I could step away, she made her own intentions clear by slipping her little hand into mine.

Wherever I went for the rest of the evening, Lisa went too—holding firmly to my hand or clinging tightly to some corner of my clothing. I tried several times—with no success—to interest her in some toy or game one of the other children was playing with. But it was soon very clear that Lisa wanted nothing more than to stick with me.

At one point a foundation staffer accompanying me whispered a warning: "I think Lisa is getting attached."

I smiled and nodded. "So am I!"

"That's not good," she cautioned.

"I know," I replied sadly. But what could I do?

When storytime came, Lisa sat first on my lap, then right at my feet, leaning against my legs, through the remaining stories. As the night wound down, I began to dread the scene I felt certain was coming. Indeed, the time finally came to bid goodbye to all the children. "I've had a wonderful time with you all tonight," I told the kids. "But it's almost time for you to be going to sleep, so Mrs. Jordan must be going now."

Lisa held on. Even when one of the counselors helped pry her hands away, she held onto me with her big brown eyes. I'll never forget those eyes.

I've thought about Lisa countless times over the past two years. Her memory still moves me.

To think that two days before I met her, this little girl was living on an icy sidewalk having known little but suffering and heartache all her life. Suddenly, as if in some incredible fairy tale, she found herself at a party in one of the world's fanciest toy stores. There, offered her choice of thousands upon thousands of the brightest, newest, most expensive toys in the entire world, Lisa longed for nothing more than a little loving attention and the reassuring warmth of a grown-up's hand.

More recently, I had another experience I want to tell you about. At a Chicago Bulls game, watching Michael play, I found myself sitting courtside with the mother of a teenage television star. When this woman learned who I was, she proudly pointed out her own son sitting in another row just a few feet away. I'd already recognized his familiar face.

This woman and I chatted cordially, off and on, as the game progressed. She seemed especially eager to talk about our shared experiences as mothers of celebrity sons. She said some gracious things about how many positive articles she'd read about Michael's character and his life off the basketball court. She seemed particularly impressed by his generosity and by the desire and need he feels (and has often publicly expressed) to reach out and give back to society—especially to those in greatest need. "You must be very proud of your son," she said.

I admitted that I was, adding that it was particularly gratifying to see how Michael had maintained so many of the basic values he'd been taught at home and church as he was growing up.

At that point this mother lowered her voice and confided that she was very concerned about her own son's moral and spiritual values. She felt that he didn't seem to have much compassion or concern for the needs of others. She said she'd tried to talk to her son recently about values and beliefs, but she didn't think she'd gotten through. "Would you be willing to talk to him, Mrs. Jordan?" she asked. "He has so much respect for Michael; maybe he'd listen to you. Please?"

What could I say? I couldn't tell her what I was thinking: *Give me a break! You expect me, a complete stranger, to somehow instantly convey to your nearly grown son a set of meaningful values and beliefs that you, as a parent, haven't managed to teach him in his seventeen years of life?*

I didn't (and still don't) want to be too hard on this woman. I recognized a desperate mother's love and concern in her eyes as she said again, "Please? It would mean so much!"

"Sure, I'll be glad to," I said. The words had barely passed my lips before she'd called her son's name and motioned the boy over. She quickly made the introductions as he knelt down beside us: "This is Mrs. Jordan, Michael's mom. I'd like you to have a chance to talk to her. You can take my seat, and I'll take yours for a little while. Okay?"

The poor boy didn't have any more options than I did.

We made small talk for a while. He seemed like a friendly and nice enough young man. He politely asked

about my family and told me a little about his. He also gave
me a quick summary of his acting career. When I inquired
about his future plans and goals in life, he seemed a bit uncertain. I then wondered aloud just how normal a life a teen
celebrity could possibly have. He explained that most of his
schoolwork was done under the supervision of a private tutor;
his work didn't allow him a regular school experience or
much time for teenage friends. He did mention that he had a
girlfriend, though.

When I asked if he managed to attend church anywhere,
he admitted that he *never* had. I told him that surprised me a
little, because his mom had expressed a real concern about
the importance of faith and values. He said he guessed that
was true for his mom, but his father had never had much use
for church or anything having to do with religion. He'd always followed his father's lead on that subject. What his dad
had taught him—and what he believed—was this: *You've always got to look out for yourself if you're going to survive in this
world, because no other being or person is going to look out for
you. And you'd better realize that everyone around you is going
to be trying to take advantage of you if you're not careful.*

Hearing such a cynical philosophy from a teenager saddened me. I tried to explain that most of the guiding principles of my life—principles I'd always tried to instill in my
family—were rooted in the moral, spiritual, and biblical values I'd learned at home and in church. The Golden Rule, for
example: "Do unto others as you would have others do unto
you" (paraphrased from Matt. 7:12). And these words of Jesus:
"It is more blessed to give than to receive" (Acts 20:35). Like-

wise, "To whom much is given, much will be required" (Matt. 13:12). I've learned from personal experience that what Jesus taught was true: the greatest sense of fulfillment we can find here on earth comes not from fame or fortune but from serving and doing things for other people.

As the basketball action raced up and down the court in front of us, I tried to say some of these things to this young man. Though he listened politely, I wasn't sure how much he was really hearing. So he surprised me when he admitted that there were times he felt something was missing in his life. And I was encouraged at the end of the game when, as we said our goodbyes and he thanked me, he added, "You've given me something to think about."

Two encounters with two children in very different circumstances. A little girl who had nothing, growing up hungry and cold on the winter streets of Chicago. A teenage boy who seemed to have everything, growing up with fame and fortune in the glamorous world of Hollywood.

Two very different children, but both with families that somehow failed to provide them with the essentials required by life. Two stories that remind me that from top to bottom of our society today, families are in crisis.

I don't presume to have all the answers. I certainly have no illusions that being the mother of the world's most famous athlete makes me a family expert. In fact, I have to admit that there are times when I've felt that being Michael's mom was an unwelcome pain.

Ray, Michael, and me in 1990 at the Michael Jordan Foundation Gala
Event raising funds to be divided among various charities.

Not long ago, during a visit to Chicago, I left my daughter Roslyn's condo to run out and pick up a few things at a nearby grocery. As I hurried in through the supermarket's front door, one of the young men bagging groceries smiled and nodded at me. When I smiled back, I saw that telltale look of uncertain recognition in his eyes. I've seen the reaction often enough to know that he thought he knew me but wasn't quite certain.

Michael's celebrity has gotten me more than my fair share of media coverage. Especially at home in the Carolinas and around Chicago, I can seldom go anywhere without someone recognizing me and wanting to talk. We'd just held our big annual fund-raising gala for the Michael Jordan Foundation a couple nights earlier; perhaps the young grocery store employee had seen one of the many television interviews I'd done for that.

How he thought he knew my face doesn't really matter; what's important is that he did. But on this particular afternoon I didn't feel much like being recognized, so I picked out a shopping cart and kept right on walking.

A minute or so later I realized I was being followed. Trying to ignore my young follower, I put a carton of orange juice in my cart and headed for another aisle. There, finally working up his nerve to approach me, the boy said, "I know who you are."

I didn't want to seem impolite, but neither did I feel like chatting. All I said in response was, "Maybe you do and maybe you don't." Then I walked to another aisle.

Suddenly he was there again. "You're Mrs. Jordan. You're Michael's mom, aren't you?"

I smiled and nodded somewhat reluctantly. "Yes, I am."

"I knew it!" he said proudly, walking excitedly toward the front of the store.

I finished my shopping as quickly as I could, but by the time I approached the checkout area, I saw the young bagger whispering to one of the cashiers and could read his lips: "There she is. That's Michael Jordan's mother." Everyone else in the front of that store, shoppers and employees alike, seemed to have heard already. They were all looking my way.

I determined to make the best of the situation, but I didn't feel very friendly at that moment. Exhausted by the weeks of planning for our foundation gala, I'd lain down and taken a short nap at Roslyn's a little earlier. On awakening, I'd hastily run a brush through my hair before heading to the store. I felt barely presentable. And now I had half the people in the store watching my every move. My quick stop for a few groceries had turned into a very public appearance.

I responded as politely as I could, trying to smile warmly while returning the greetings of all the people who now felt obliged to speak to me before I could pay my bill and escape to the parking lot and the welcome privacy of my car. However, I felt very put upon that afternoon. By the time I got back to Roslyn's, I'd worked up enough irritation that I needed to let off a little steam; so I told my daughter exactly what had happened. I expected a little empathy, because I knew Ros had been in numerous similar situations when she hadn't welcomed the public's attention. In fact, she'd voiced her own frustration about being recognized as "Michael's sister" on more than one occasion.

But on this particular afternoon, I didn't get the sympathetic response I had expected. Instead, my younger daughter, who often seems to have grown spiritually sensitive and wise beyond her years, offered me this advice: "You know, Mother," she said, "I think maybe you need to see every incident like this afternoon as a special blessing, a special opportunity God has given you to reach out and touch other people, to encourage them and make a difference in their lives."

My first thought was, *O Lord, please don't give me so many blessings! I didn't ask for any special opportunities.*

In my heart, however, I instantly knew Roslyn was right. But still this question remained: *How can you turn an awkward, sometimes unwanted encounter into a positive, encouraging experience?*

Actually, some people I meet in public make that easy by saying gracious things such as, "Michael played a great game last night. I know that made you proud," or "I've always been a big fan of your son's, so it's very nice to meet you. I wish you and your family the best." I seldom mind those who stop me on the street or in a restaurant to shake hands and offer a simple, quick greeting such as, "It's nice to meet you, Mrs. Jordan. I'll be rooting for the Bulls tonight," or "It's nice to see you here today, Mrs. Jordan."

It's those people who want to monopolize my attention by rambling on and on while my food gets cold or my time slips away that present a real annoyance. And those who leave

Michael's kindergarten photo, Roslyn's kindergarten photo

Ronnie's 11th grade ROTC photo, Larry's 1st grade photo

Delois's 4th grade photo. All are school pictures.

the conversational ball in my court by asking silly or awkward questions. How is a mother expected to respond, for example, when someone asks (and people have), "Is Michael really as nice a person off the court as all the articles say he is?" Do people expect me to say, "That's all just PR hype. He's not a very nice human being at all"? And how about those people who stop me to ask, "What was wrong with Michael last night? He scored only twenty-nine points and missed three out of four shots in the last minute of the game." Do they expect me to offer some armchair analysis and second-guess my own son? There are more than enough commentators and sports columnists anxious to do that.

So how can I do what Roslyn suggested and turn these unsought public encounters into meaningful opportunities to encourage and help others? When I pressed her, Roslyn admitted that it wouldn't always be easy.

"Whenever someone approaches you, maybe you could respond by quoting Scripture," she suggested. We both laughed to think how quickly some people might flee if they heard me spouting Bible verses and threatening to launch into a sermon.

But the more Ros and I talked that afternoon, the more I realized there are often things I might say to help and encourage some of the people who approach me in public merely because I'm "Michael Jordan's mother." I vowed to work at the challenge my daughter had spelled out for me; I determined to think ahead and plan what I could say.

For example, when people walk up to me to say what a wonderful basketball player my son is, I might say something like this: "Yes, Michael is a terrific basketball player. I'm very proud of the way he's used the great athletic skills God has given him. But I'm even more proud of the kind of person he is off the court, because in the long run, in the light of eternity, that's far more important than a game or even a career."

And when people praise my son's basketball skills— especially young people—I need to make a point of saying, "You're right. Michael has been blessed with some amazing athletic potential. But you know, he's really had to work over the years to sharpen those skills and achieve his potential. The truth is our Creator has made each of us with our own special talents and abilities, and he wants each of us to work hard to reach our God-given potential. It's not often easy. I hope you understand that doing your best always takes effort. But I wish you well in all that you do."

I don't expect that responses like these will make a life-changing impact on everyone I meet. But perhaps they'll leave people with a thought that God can then use to shape or alter their thinking and their attitudes. I may never know.

I do know, though, that when I can think to say something intentionally positive to the people who approach me, it sheds a whole new light on these awkward, sometimes unwanted encounters. Then they truly seem like God-given blessings and opportunities.

And the more I've been thinking about this lesson my daughter helped me learn, the more I see the connection to this book. I was asked to write it (and you probably picked it up and began reading it) primarily because I'm "Michael's mom."

I'm comfortable with that. In fact, 99.9 percent of the time I'm proud to be known as "Michael's mom." It's not a role I chose. God gave it to me. With it has come an incredible God-given opportunity to say something here on these pages that will encourage and help others in their family roles.

I'm well aware that being "Michael's mom" is what gives me this extraordinary platform. But I want you to understand that it's my very ordinary experience as the mother of five children that has provided me with any worthwhile wisdom I might have to share about parenting, motherhood, child-rearing, and the incredible importance of family in our society today.

Much has been written about the Jordan family already. Some of it is even true! But the primary purpose of the personal stories I tell here is not to set the record straight. It's merely one mother's attempt to share what wisdom she's gained in almost forty years of parenting.

I'm writing because I've seen the need for and the importance of families. I'm writing because God has allowed me a very special platform that I feel obliged to use.

Yes, I'm Michael Jordan's mother. I do have a world-famous son. But I had a family first. And putting family first is what I write about in the rest of this book.

2

When asked to speak at schools or in some other setting where I encounter young people, I'm often amused by the questions kids ask me. One that comes up frequently is some variation of this: "When he was growing up, did you ever give Michael a whippin'?"

"Why, of course!" I say. "Mr. Jordan and I had to spank each of our children on numerous occasions."

My affirmative answer to this punishment question almost always meets with the same sequence of reactions from my questioners. First there's a surprised look of disbelief, a momentary inability to imagine their larger-than-life athletic hero ever getting a spanking (let alone from this rather unimposing woman standing in front of them). Sometimes I see that initial expression of disbelief slowly shift to a sort of grudging respect as the truth sinks in and they realize that I am, after all—and always will be—Michael's mother. And finally, when I confess to having physically punished all my children at one point or another, I often witness at least a small measure of disappointment on the face or in the eyes of the young person who asked me the question.

This last reaction could be the natural result of reality dawning as the kids begin to understand that their hero is in fact very human. But I've often suspected that the disappointment is a little more practical and personal. Many of the questioners are probably hoping for arguments and ammunition that will change their own parents' minds about child-rearing strategies: "Michael Jordan's mother says he never got a spanking, and look how he turned out!"

Kids, like the rest of us, don't always want to hear the truth about their heroes.

I remember an incident that happened during the first year or so of Michael's NBA career, when he was just beginning to acquire his now-widespread fame. Diane Sawyer, along with her network camera crew, showed up at Michael's townhouse for a scheduled interview only to find him hurriedly vacuuming the living room. When she reacted with genuine surprise, Michael explained that he was rushing to finish cleaning up not because a television crew was going to film him at home but because he wanted to have everything looking nice before his mother arrived for a visit later that afternoon. On camera, Diane Sawyer marveled that a rich, young bachelor basketball star would be doing his own vacuuming rather than leaving all the cleanup to a maid service he could obviously afford. Michael explained to Diane and her viewers that he'd always been required to clean his room, make his bed, do dishes, help with laundry, and carry out his share of

Family photo, circa 1972.

the family's household chores. As a result of such parental expectations, he felt very capable of taking care of himself now that he was out on his own. Chores were just a natural and necessary part of life.

When that interview aired, Michael received a pile of complaint mail from kids. "Why did you have to be vacuuming your house when the TV crew showed up? Why did you have to say what you did about chores? Now my mom is always saying, 'If Michael Jordan can do housework, so can you.' Thanks a lot, Michael! I've got more chores than ever because of you."

Kids aren't the only ones with more of a tendency to glamorize a public figure than to humanize him. Indeed, many of the adults I speak with and meet seem to find it hard to grasp the reality that someone who is an extraordinary athlete and celebrity could come from a very ordinary family. So it seems that the Jordan family has received unsought attention and notoriety because of, and undue credit for, Michael's achievements and celebrity.

Many are the times that I've had to shake my head in amazement at all that has happened to me and my family simply because of our relationship to Michael—so many interviews, so many honors and awards. One of my most unbelievable experiences came in Chicago when I, in recognition for our foundation's work with children and our support of UNICEF, was named the 1992 recipient of UNICEF's World of Children Award, presented at a black-tie, high-society gala entitled "An Evening with Audrey Hepburn." Sitting on the dais that evening, looking at the list of people who were previous recipients of this award—people such as Audrey Hepburn, Maggie Daley, Harry Belafonte, Peter Ustinov, Father Theodore Hesburgh, and Lillian Carter—I thought, *What in the world am I doing up here?* I had much the same need to pinch myself back in 1990, when I learned that *Esquire* magazine had chosen me to appear in a special issue featuring "women we love." When my picture appeared amidst all those air-brushed shots of glamorous young media stars and celebrities, I could only shake my head in disbelief. But I did feel good about the caption, which said, "Nobody else has successfully covered her baby Michael since she tucked him in. She gave him humility, business sense, and an occasional whack on the butt. No matter how high he now flies, she can always bring him back to earth."

But there's a downside to public recognition and awards. They can make it more difficult for people to relate to our family experience and to my experience as a parent and mother. That means I have to work even harder to remind people that my husband and I didn't set out to raise a world-famous superstar. We simply set out to raise a family—in the best way we knew how.

To understand what I have to say about family and parenthood, and the context in which I've lived and learned it, you need a quick summary of the Jordan family history.

Appropriately enough, it was at a basketball game that I first met James Raymond Jordan. (While most people knew him as James Jordan, I always called him Ray.) He played at

Charity High School in rural Wallace, North Carolina, and competed against my older brothers, Edward and Eugene Peoples, at Pender County Training School outside Wilmington.

One winter night in 1954, after a Pender County win over Charity High, my cousins and I joined a carload of kids hitching a ride home with Ray. I don't think he knew who I was, or even that I'd gotten into his car, until he zoomed past my house and I screamed in panic for him to stop and let me out.

As I climbed out of the car, Ray looked up and grinned: "And who's this cute little thing?" he asked. When I responded rather indignantly, letting him know I thought he was being fresh, he laughed and said, "That's okay, honey. One day I'm going to marry you!"

That comment so surprised and flustered me that I bolted out of the car and didn't stop running until I'd slammed the front door of my house behind me. Soon after that, Ray set out to make his marriage prophecy come true by showing up at my house to ask my father if he could take me out. Dad said no at first, but Ray's persistence paid off.

We quickly fell in love and dated steadily for the next three years. After Ray graduated from school, joined the Air Force, and shipped out to San Antonio, my parents packed me up and sent me off to live with my uncle in Alabama, where I was to take a two-year cosmetology program at the Tuskegee Trade Institute. I think my mom was hoping to put some time and distance between Ray and me and to give me a chance to grow up and see a little bit of the big wide world beyond coastal North Carolina. One year in Alabama, though—away from home and away from Ray—was enough to convince me that what I wanted most in life was to become Mrs. James Raymond Jordan and begin a family with the first and only man I'd ever loved. I returned home one weekend to find Ray home on leave, and I never went back to Tuskegee.

Ray soon got transferred to a base in nearby Virginia, we got married, and I moved to Wallace to live with his parents while he commuted home on weekends whenever he could. We were just kids, totally unprepared for parenthood. But we were so much in love that when our first child was born the following year, I decided to name him James Ronald (we called him Ronnie), after my husband and in recognition of the shared excitement of this event, which seemed so significant to both of us. Ray decided not to re-up with the Air Force the following year and had just come out of the service when our first daughter was born. Since I'd named our son after him, Ray wanted to name her Delois, a variation on my name. (We did, but within the family we called her Sis.)

Ray went to work for the J. P. Stevens textile mill, the only major employer in or around Wallace; and we built a little house, the first home of our own, right across the road from his parents'. By the time our third child, Larry, was born another three years later, Ray and I both were beginning to dream of a better life beyond Wallace. Ray had always been good with his hands, and in the military he'd maintained and repaired airplanes. When he decided that what he needed in order to find a more promising career was some formal training in a field using those skills, we boarded up our home and moved to New York City for almost two years. There Ray attended a trade school on the G.I. Bill and learned to build, repair, and service hydraulic equipment. Michael was born while we lived in New York, and our younger daughter, Roslyn, was born the following year, after we'd returned to North Carolina.

Wallace seemed more confining than ever after two years in New York. We soon decided to sell our home and move to the "big city" of Wilmington. There Ray landed a job doing machine maintenance at the local GE plant, which manufactured aircraft parts. Before long he got promoted to supervisor and eventually became parts manager, with responsibility for the purchase, distribution, and maintenance of the equipment parts needed to keep the entire plant's production machinery up and running.

And so it was in the beautiful, historic seaport town of Wilmington, North Carolina, that we settled down, made our home, and raised our family for nineteen short and wonderful years.

In truth, we had what seemed a very ordinary family— one very much like other working-class and middle-class families living then (or today) in rural and small-town North Carolina. Like most of our neighbors, we constantly struggled with the reality and limitations of a tight budget—trying to figure out what corners to cut, what bills to hold until the next month so that we could pay the extra cost of a field trip, a Girl Scout uniform, or a basketball camp. Like every parent I've ever talked to, we wondered how and where we could carve out the extra time to take our kids to one more cheerleading tryout, club meeting, band practice, or ballgame. Then, when our children reached that terrifying age

Ronnie and Delois, in the
Easter program at Church
on Easter Sunday 1964

of sixteen and could drive themselves where they needed to be, we paced the floor worrying until they finally got home or, if they weren't home by curfew, went out searching for them. Like the parents of teenagers everywhere, we worried and prayed about the dangers and temptations facing each of our children—dating, peer pressure, motivation in school, alcohol, and drugs. As parents have done for generation after generation, from the beginning of our children's lives we dreamed of the day when each of the kids would be able to leave home and enter the world to find an easier, brighter, more productive, and more fulfilling life than we had lived. And we longed to provide the solid foundation on which they could begin to build that dream.

How did we seek to do that? What did the Jordans learn in the process? That's what the remainder of this book is about.

Before we move on to the heart of this book, I want to mention two fundamental prerequisites that I think are absolutely crucial to any discussion of family or parenting today. On the one hand, they seem so basic and undeniable that I feel I shouldn't have to bring them up. On the other hand, they seem to be troubling enough to warrant attention: in my travels and in my speaking, I encounter two attitudes so frequently that I have to conclude there's a disturbing lack of understanding and perspective among many parents today in these two critical and related areas.

The first and more common of these two troubling attitudes shows up time and again when I hear parents young and old complain, "It's so hard being a mother [or father] today!"

I know that most people who complain about the difficulty of parenthood are probably looking for a little sympathy—or at least empathy. But sometimes I feel like looking them right in the eyes and saying, "What did you expect? What gave you the idea parenting would be simple? I don't know any good parents who ever thought it was easy."

Erma Bombeck, in her 1989 book *I Want to Grow Hair, I Want to Grow Up, I Want to Go to Boise: Children Surviving Cancer,* imagined the following newspaper advertisement for the position of motherhood. "Wanted: Woman to raise, educate, and entertain child for a minimum of 20 years. Be prepared to eat egg if the yoke breaks, receive anything in hand the child spits out, and take knots out of wet shoestrings with teeth. Must be expert in making costume for bad tooth and picking locks with shishkebab skewer. Seven days a week, 24 hours a day, including holidays. Comprehensive dental plan, vacation, medical benefits and company car negotiable."

An alarming number of parents today seem completely blindsided by, or at least woefully unprepared for, the incredible demands of the job. What I find even more disturbing is the number who then are reluctant or unable to make the effort required by the responsibilities.

Commitment is what we're talking about here. If you're not ready and willing to talk about commitment, I don't think you're ready to talk about parenthood. Commitment is a prerequisite for everything I have to say about parenthood. Every basic family-building tool and parenting strategy I address later in this book requires a large measure of commitment.

Successful families demand it. Good parenting begins and ends with it.

As troubled as I am to hear parents lament the commitment required by the job, I think I have an even harder time with a second pervasive attitude. I see it in those parents who corner me after I speak somewhere or who stop me in a mall, an airport, or some other public place only to ramble on and on in an attempt to impress me with the athletic prowess or potential of their child, who they are convinced is going to be (in their words) "the next Michael Jordan." I'm even more appalled by those parents who tell me how they demand that their athletically gifted son practice his sport so many hours a day, how they send him to this sports camp and that sports camp, how no sacrifice is too great in their pursuit of athletic success, because "one day my son will be a superstar, make big money, and take care of me."

I can't count the number of times I've had people say something like that to me. And every time I hear it, I want to scream, "That's child abuse!" I truly think it is.

These parents lack the second critical prerequisite of parenthood—a clear and healthy *vision*, an understanding of the proper roles and goals of parenthood and family.

Every parent has dreams and goals for his or her children. Ray and I certainly did.

Sometimes on miserably hot and sticky summer nights, when the kids were safe and asleep in their rooms, Ray and I would slip out of the house and make the five-mile drive out to Wrightsville Beach. Sometimes we'd walk hand in hand through the dunes; other times we'd just sit in our moonlit car, enjoying the cool breeze off the Atlantic Ocean and talking about our children and the dreams we shared for them. Never once did we discuss the possibility that one of our children would become a rich or famous athletic superstar.

As I said before, we didn't set out to raise a superstar. I think anyone who makes that his or her parental goal has a tragically misguided vision of parenthood. In fact, I believe parents are treading on dangerous ground anytime they see their children's "success" or achievement in any field as their goal and purpose in parenthood.

Then what sort of goals should families and parents have for their children?

Character goals! We'll look at some specifics and talk about what our family did to pursue those goals later in this book.

Commitment and *vision*. Two prerequisites of parenthood. Two themes that will be woven through the very fabric of our discussion of parenthood, making children a priority, and putting family first.

The drive from Wilmington to the University of North Carolina campus took us between two and three hours. Whenever the Tarheels played at home, Ray and I could get off work a few minutes early, head for Chapel Hill, grab a fast-food meal on the way, and arrive at the old Carmichael Coliseum in plenty of time to watch Michael and his teammates finish their warm-up.

But one game night during Michael's junior year, the weather turned ugly and traffic around Raleigh-Durham got so bad that we were running late. "We're not going to make tip-off, are we?" I asked Ray.

"I don't think so," he admitted. "But we should be close."

We pulled into the parking lot just about the time the game was scheduled to begin. "If we hurry, we won't miss much!" Ray exclaimed as we jumped out of the car and raced for the stadium entrance.

Michael, Ray, and me at the University of
North Carolina at Chapel Hill in 1982

When we burst through the front door and into the lobby, there—much to our surprise—stood UNC's assistant coach Eddie Fogler.

"You're here!" he greeted us, obviously relieved.

"We got stuck in traffic, and—" Ray began to explain.

"Let's go," Eddie interrupted as he ushered us toward the doors into the stadium itself. "We haven't started the game yet. We were waiting for you."

"You were *what?*" I couldn't believe I'd heard him right.

"When Michael spotted your empty seats, he started asking if anyone had seen you. Coach Smith didn't want to start the game with Michael so worried, so we decided to delay the tip-off as long as we could."

Thousands of psyched-up Carolina fans packed into that stadium, along with viewers in a statewide television audience, were all kept waiting because we got stuck in traffic! I didn't want to believe it. But I knew it was true—because Eddie Fogler had been anxiously watching for us, and because Michael looked up and smiled as we slipped into our seats. Moments later the horn sounded and the team broke the huddle to walk out on the floor for the opening tip. As far as I know, the reason for the delay was never made public. We certainly didn't tell anyone. But Ray and I did make sure we allowed a little extra travel time to get to Chapel Hill the rest of that season!

Why would Coach Dean Smith delay the start of a basketball game for a single set of parents? He realized how upset Michael was. And why was Michael so worried by our empty seats? Because we had made it a lifelong practice to be there when Michael or any of our other children played a game or performed in public. The only way we wouldn't be there was if something was wrong. Since Michael knew that, he had good reason to worry.

For Ray and me, *being there* was always an essential and required parenting strategy. It didn't begin with college basketball games or with our fourth child. It was a lifelong commitment we made to each of our five children. Because this sort of commitment is so important, whenever I speak to parents today I emphasize the importance of *being there* for their children. It's what I talk about in this chapter.

This seems to be such a simple, basic idea that I often ask myself, *Do I really need to say this again? Don't parents realize this already?*

Then I get a request like the one I received recently from the Chicago Public Schools, asking me to make a special public service announcement for them. It seems that a few years ago the Chicago school board established a revolutionary new policy in an attempt to encourage more parents to become at least minimally involved in their children's education. Instead of sending report cards home with students for a parent to sign, the district now requires parents to come to the school once every six weeks to personally pick up each child's report card from the teacher.

The trouble is this: at the end of the first six-week grading period of the 1995–96 schoolyear, the parents of more than 40,000 Chicago students failed to pick up their kids' report cards on the assigned date. Across the city a staggering total of 25,000 report cards went uncollected and unsigned. To fight this apparent apathy, the Chicago school system recruited me to make a special public service announcement to run on local television at the end of the second grading period.

On camera I said these words:

Hi, I'm the mother of five. One of my children you know quite well: Michael. Mr. Jordan and I always made a point of being involved in each of our children's education. Every principal, teacher, and counselor knew they could call on us for support.

Do you know how your child is doing in class? You can find out on November 15 and 16. These are report card pickup days for Chicago's public schools.

Please get more involved as a parent. You can meet your child's teachers, discuss report cards, and make a big contribution to your child's education.

It's "Children First" in all Chicago schools. So please be in class on November 15 for elementary grades and/or November 16 for high school. It's the best possible investment in your child's future.

I know my family would agree.

I was happy to film the PSA, but I couldn't help thinking how sad it is that we have to resort to sixty-second television spots pleading with parents to care enough to find out how their children are doing in school.

Just think! In one city there are 25,000 kids whose parents (that's 50,000 of them) weren't willing or able to make the effort to get involved—even on such a minimal level. Since I doubt the Chicago school system is unique on this score, it's probably safe to assume there are millions of parents in thousands of other cities and towns across the country who need to be reminded of the importance of involvement in their kids' lives. For involvement is a large part of what I'm talking about when I address parents on the importance of *being there* for their children.

Let me hasten to say that it's not just inner-city kids or disadvantaged children whose parents need this message. In my travel, my speaking, and my work with the Michael Jordan Foundation, I encounter a disturbing number of upper-middle-class and well-to-do parents, including many professional people, who seem uninvolved in the daily lives of their children.

When they tell me about "the most wonderful nanny" they found for their children so that both husband and wife can pursue demanding careers, I'm tempted to ask, "Who's really raising your children? Who's there to applaud your son's first steps? Who does your daughter run to for comfort when she falls and skins her knee? Who do your children expect to *be there*?"

Many of these same parents admit to me that their careers and their pressing personal schedules prevent them from spending as much time as they would like with their children. "But what I don't have in *quantity time*," they say, "I make up for with *quality time*."

When I hear that, I generally want to say, "I think that's a cop-out!"

Don't get me wrong. I'm a strong believer in and a frequent proponent of "quality time." Most parents need to make a more concerted effort to plan for and provide greater opportunity for meaningful quality time with their children. And the less time parents spend with their children, for whatever the reason—whether it's the regular responsibilities of a demanding job, frequent travel, or the stresses of a broken marriage—the more crucial quality time is.

But let's be honest! Quality time can't completely make up for lost quantity time. The two aren't truly interchangeable; they aren't the same thing.

Quantity time often *leads* to quality time, however. It's what *being there* is all about.

Whether it's a baby uttering precious first words or a child coming home from school in tears over the unkind words of a friend, a parent can't share that special moment or meet that immediate need without *being there*. In fact, many of the most memorable and crucial quality times parents have with children can't be scheduled. They just happen. To some degree, then, the more quantity time we spend with our children, the better the chances we'll be there at the most significant quality times in their lives.

I'm not attempting to create unnecessary guilt here. None of us can or should spend twenty-four hours a day, seven days a week, with our children. I know very well that jobs and other responsibilities demand parents' time. I also know that some family circumstances separate parents and children for long periods of time. In those circumstances, a conscientious pursuit of quality time helps compensate for the loss of quantity time.

But we need to be honest enough to admit that it's *only* compensation. Quality time, as important as it is, never quite makes up for the importance of *being there*.

The value of *being there* seems most obvious when our children are young. I vividly remember the almost overwhelming sense of responsibility I felt when I first looked at Ronnie, with his eyes scrunched shut in his fat little newborn face. I felt the same way when I first took my daughter Delois in my arms—and then again and again and again after the births of Larry, Michael, and Roslyn.

Whenever I held one of my newborn children, I was struck by the infant's total helplessness. I remember the sobering realization that *this child will know only what I as a parent provide for him. Who and what he becomes will be decided by the foundation I lay.*

It's an awesome, frightening power that parents are granted. And yet most of us happily accept that responsibility. We're excited to become parents—with everything that means. And whenever we hold, cuddle, rock, and nurse our little ones, we're ready and willing to be there as an important part of their lives forever.

As our children grow and become less helpless, the chemistry changes. We can't and shouldn't be involved in their lives in the same way. And yet *being there* remains vitally important.

I learned part of this lesson by trial and error. Once Michael and Ros started school, I decided I could ease some of the family's financial pressure by getting a full-time paying job. I soon landed a position at the local Corning Glass Works plant, which manufactured electronic television parts.

While working on an assembly line wasn't the most thrilling job in the world, I enjoyed the friendships and camaraderie that came with being part of a team. I found personal satisfaction in doing my job quickly and efficiently. I felt affirmed when my work earned me a promotion and I was given added responsibility for quality control. And with five growing children, Ray and I both appreciated the additional family income.

The biggest problem with my job was that it was shift work. One week I'd be scheduled to work days, the next week evenings, and the following week nights. The constant change wreaked havoc on the family schedule. For a while I traded off with other Corning employees whenever I could, in order to work days. But since most of my co-workers preferred to work normal daytime hours, and since consistency benefited family scheduling, I began working mostly evenings.

That way I was available in the mornings to get the kids off to school and could get supper started cooking before I left for work at about the time they arrived home. When Ray returned home a little later, he finished preparing supper and then served it, supervised homework, and bathed and readied the children for bed. I got home exhausted a little before midnight, wishing I had a few extra hours before the whole thing started over again the next morning.

This schedule gave me mornings and weekends with my children. Working evenings even allowed me to regularly volunteer to read and help out in other ways at their schools. But I never could shake the feeling that I was missing a lot by not *being there* with my kids every afternoon and evening—prime time for most family relationships.

I'll always remember the sense of relief—the tangible feeling of peace—I experienced the day I walked into the Corning plant, handed in my uniform and my security badge, then turned right around and went back home. I hadn't gotten up that morning thinking, *This is the day I'm going to quit.* Though I'd been seriously considering the option for some time, and I'd discussed the possibility with Ray, the final decision came very suddenly. I knew what I had to do: I wanted to *be there* for my kids in ways that my job didn't allow.

"What are *you* doing here?" Ray asked in surprise when he got home that afternoon.

"I quit my job today."

I'll forever be grateful for Ray's accepting and supportive response. "Okay," he said. He never once questioned the wisdom or the timing of my decision. He didn't once ask me to reconsider or try to talk me into going back. He didn't protest or complain about the drastic and immediate implications my decision would have for our family budget. He didn't even ask me why I'd suddenly decided to quit; he knew, because we'd talked about my feelings.

Ray's response affirmed me. It reminded me that he valued what I did for our children. It encouraged me, because it showed me in yet another way what I'd always felt: when it came to family and parenting, we were a team. We both believed in the importance of *being there* for our kids. And he understood how hard it was for me to be there emotionally for our children when I wasn't there physically.

For Ray, being a dependable provider was a big part of *being there* for his family. I was always grateful for that and tried to let him know it. There were times when his job kept him from being at home with the family, especially after he became a supervisor. For example, problems at the plant sometimes required his presence after hours, or an assembly-line breakdown might force him to charter a plane and fly halfway across the country in the middle of the night to acquire the one crucial part required to get the plant back online the next day. But those emergencies, those absent times, were the exception. Ray was usually there with the family— for supper, to check homework, to play catch in the yard, and to share the highlights of his day with me once we got the kids settled in bed.

When I decided to go back to work again a few years later, I remembered the difficult lesson I'd learned at Corning. As a teller at a branch of the United Carolina Bank, I was able to get my children off to school in the mornings and still be home soon after school ended in the afternoon. Even after I got promoted to our bank headquarters downtown as a customer service representative, I always had an understanding with my bosses. If I worked straight through my assigned coffee and lunch breaks, I could leave early enough in the afternoon to pick up the kids from any of their after-school activities. And whenever I did take a lunch break—maybe once a week—I scheduled it so that I could run out to the elementary school to have lunch with one of my children or volunteer a little help with a reading group in one of their classrooms.

For both Ray and me, *being there* for our kids meant more than spending family time together at home. It required involvement in our kids' lives away from home as well.

Whether it was church and Sunday school on Sunday mornings or baseball practice out at the Optimist Club fields during the week, neither Ray nor I was content simply to drop our kids off and go our own way. We saw lots of families who did. But for us, *being there* required more than taxi service from one activity to another. If our children participated in any activity, we were also involved. Whether it was Sis taking part in a school play or the annual church Christmas program or Ronnie marching in a Fourth of July parade with his Junior ROTC unit, we were there when our children performed. Whenever and wherever Larry and Michael played a game, whether it was a regular season contest at the park down the road from our house or a state championship baseball tournament at the other end of the state, Ray and I (and usually the rest of the kids as well) made the trip to be in the stands cheering and rooting for our sons. When Ros's Girl Scout troop held a fund-raiser, I went with her before dawn on Saturday morning to pick up the doughnuts she needed to sell. When the Laney High Boosters Club decided to build a new ballfield, Ray worked from morning to night helping clear the land.

And in all those years raising five children, I don't think either of us ever gave this kind of involvement a second thought. We never discussed whether or not we could make such commitments. It's what we expected—from ourselves and from each other. For us, it was all part of *being there* for and with our kids.

While a lot of discouraging things have been written and said about the alarming state of the family in our society today, in my speaking and my work with our foundation I've come to the heartening conclusion that there are literally millions and millions of parents across America who are committed to *being there* for their children—devoted, well-meaning parents who understand the importance of getting involved in their children's lives. They're willing, able, and ready to take that responsibility.

What discourages me is that so many of these same parents seem to burn out and abdicate that responsibility far too soon. If you talk to educators anywhere in the country, you'll hear the same story: the older their students, the harder it is to keep parents involved in the educational process. The folks in Chicago who asked me to make the PSA said that this was true at report card time; the older the students, the higher the percentage of parents who failed to come in to learn how their kids were doing.

When kindergarten classes have a PTA program, parents turn out in droves. It's much harder to get the parents of middle schoolers out to a program, and even fewer parents get involved at the high school level. By the time most parents drop their college freshmen off on campus, the vast majority seem to assume that their active role in the educational life of their children is over.

It concerns me that so many parents today seem to believe that the importance of *being there* has a time limit. My experience tells me it doesn't.

For example, my children had friends who graduated from high school only to learn that they didn't have all the credits required to get into college. If their parents had been there to ask questions and help make sure they understood the requirements, those kids wouldn't have had to attend summer school or go back to high school for an extra semester before they could get accepted into college.

To be sure, the parents of a high school or college student can't and shouldn't *be there* in the same way they were when the child was a preschooler. The nature of our involvement needs to change, but the basic need remains the same. Our children never outgrow their need for us to be there for them. (In Chapter 4, we'll consider some of the ever-evolving adjustments parents have to make.)

Think for a minute. At what point in their lives are our children most vulnerable to the temptations of the world and to the negative influence of those around them? When do they make the most serious and significant decisions of their lives? In their teenage and college years.

And when do most parents decide to reduce (and sometimes abandon) their attempts at involvement in their children's lives? In their teenage and college years.

This means millions of us mothers and fathers are abdicating our parental responsibility at the most critical time in our children's lives. I realize we're talking now about the basic and age-old conflict of adolescence: the inclination of parents to hang on too long and too tightly versus the child's natural and healthy desire for independence. But I'm convinced that in our attempt to avoid unpleasant parent/teen conflict and foster the adult independence we genuinely want for our children, too many parents today are letting go too soon and too suddenly.

We'll talk more about "loosening the grip" later. Here I just want to acknowledge that knowing when and how to *be there* for our kids as they grow and mature presents one of the most difficult and important challenges of parenthood.

I remember when Michael played football his freshman year of high school. All his life he'd competed in sports against his older brother Larry and other older kids in the community. While that practice against more experienced competition always served him well in baseball and basketball, I worried that my skinny ninth-grade son might not hold up quite as well playing football against bigger, stronger, older foes.

"Don't worry. I'll be okay, Mom," he assured me whenever I voiced my concern. "But if I ever *do* get hurt, you have to promise me you won't come out on the field to check on me."

"Are you crazy?" I responded. "Of *course* I'll be out there. You're my son."

"No, Mother. Please!" he pleaded. "It would be too embarrassing."

Michael suited up for football in 10th grade at Laney High School

"Okay," I promised reluctantly, praying that the situation would never come up.

Not long after that I arrived at Michael's JV game a few minutes after kickoff. I quickly spotted Michael sitting on the sidelines and wondered why he wasn't in the game. Soon a nearby spectator leaned over and said something about hoping Michael would be all right.

"What?" I asked, perplexed.

"Michael got injured a few plays ago. Didn't you know? They're waiting for an ambulance to transport him to the hospital."

It was all I could do to keep from jumping from the stands and racing out to the bench. But remembering my promise, I stood up and walked as calmly as I could to my car. Then I drove to the hospital and was there waiting when my son arrived by ambulance for treatment of a separated shoulder. And from the welcome look I saw in Michael's eyes when the paramedics wheeled him into that emergency room, I don't think he was a bit embarrassed by my being there.

Certainly we have to make major adjustments in our parenting role as our children grow and develop. But we do have a continuing role to play.

By the time Michael went off to college, we'd established such a long pattern of *being there* for him and all of our other kids that Ray and I just assumed we'd attend all of his University of North Carolina basketball games. And we did. Home and away. Including big annual road trips to the West Coast, a tournament in Hawaii, the NCAA regionals, the Final Four, and one wonderfully memorable exhibition tour of Greece.

This involvement took some careful and creative financial planning, but we never once questioned whether or not we would or should make that kind of commitment. Not only did Ray and I want and expect to be there, but by this time in Michael's life he also expected us to be there whenever he played. And he let us know in a variety of ways that our presence wasn't just something he tolerated; it was *appreciated*.

I remember the one and only game I missed during Michael's three-year collegiate career. Though I'd been sick at home in bed with the flu all day, I tried to get up and dressed in time to drive to Chapel Hill with Ray. But it was no use: as much as I wanted to go, I was just too sick. I stayed home in bed and sent Ray on to the game alone. He got a message passed to Michael before the game started, to let him know why I wasn't there. But within minutes of the game's exciting conclusion (North Carolina won in overtime), Michael called home.

"Are you okay, Mom?" he wanted to know.

"Didn't your dad tell you?"

"He said you had the flu."

"I do. But I watched the whole game on TV. You did great!"

"Thanks, Mom. But are you sure you're going to be okay? I was worried about you."

I found it reassuring that my All-American son seemed so concerned when I wasn't able to be there for one of his college games.

When Michael opted to leave college and turn pro after his junior year, I initially opposed his decision. I not only wanted him to get his degree, but I also worried that he wasn't quite ready to handle the pressures and requirements of a professional career.

As draft day approached and it looked certain he'd be selected by either Portland or Chicago, I hoped for the Trailblazers. As far as it was to Oregon, as difficult as it would be for us to stay closely involved in his life on the West Coast, I thought life in Portland would seem an easier adjustment for a small-town boy from North Carolina.

But we'll never know what might have been, because Portland took the University of Kentucky center Sam Bowie, the Chicago Bulls drafted Michael, and I was suddenly faced with a dilemma. How were we going to redefine *being there* for Michael now that he was out of college, an instant millionaire, and living and working in a major city hundreds of miles away?

Ray and I had a lot of long, serious discussions, both between ourselves and with Michael. We all knew that we'd come to a major fork in the road. We could no longer *be there* for him the same way we had when he'd lived at home or even when he'd been in college.

No doubt some people would conclude that there was no way to continue to be there for Michael in a physical sense, that it was time to pack him up and send him on his way, contenting ourselves now with offering long-distance emotional support and encouragement. But I couldn't do that.

As mature and responsible as I knew my son was, I kept thinking, *He's only nineteen years old. He's not ready to be cut loose to make his own way alone in a big city like Chicago!*

So what did we do? I took time off from the bank and went to Chicago with Michael. The Bulls put him up in a hotel near their practice facilities to begin with, but he and I found a townhouse he wanted to buy in a nearby suburb. My banking experience came in handy for helping with the real estate business. And once Michael closed on the townhouse, my homemaking experience came into play.

While Michael was away at practice and working out with the Bulls each day, I went shopping for necessary household items and furnishings for his new home. That proved to be an education for both of us: I soon learned that my young-adult son and I had very different taste in furniture.

While I usually liked a traditional look, Michael clearly preferred a more contemporary decor. On more than one occasion he asked me to return some piece of furniture I'd bought, because he didn't like it. I remember him saying, "You bought that for *you*, Mom. It's the kind of thing you like, and it's nice. But that's just not what *I* want."

I had to admit he was right. And I knew I needed to respect his wishes and accept his taste in interior decorating.

I eventually resigned from my bank position and remained in Chicago with Michael until after the regular NBA season began that November of 1984. At that point, with him comfortably settled in his own place and gone on road trips with the Bulls half of every month anyway, it seemed time for me to return to North Carolina. And yet Ray and I didn't want to let go completely quite yet.

For the next five or six months—the rest of Michael's rookie season—whenever the Bulls were at home in Chicago, Ray or I (or both of us) would try to be there with him. When one of us couldn't manage to get away, Michael generally called and asked one of his brothers or sisters to come for a visit.

Some people would probably think we were being too protective, too controlling. But we knew that Michael's unique position as a professional basketball star would mean pressures, opportunities, temptations, and decisions that no nineteen-year-old boy could be fully prepared to face. With so many huge adjustments for him to make, it just didn't seem the time or the place to suddenly remove the lifelong support system we'd always tried to provide by *being there* for our son. And I've never regretted the effort our family made to *be there* for Michael his rookie season.

Things had changed by the next year. Although we visited Chicago often, we knew that Michael would do fine on his own. Yet I'm convinced we all needed that one year of transition and adjustment, that period when we made an extra effort to stay involved in our son's life on a regular, daily basis.

Many of the feelings and issues Ray and I experienced during Michael's rookie year we relived again a few years later when Roslyn told us she wanted to move to Southern California. She'd lived on her own and worked in banking in the Chapel Hill area for a couple years after she graduated from UNC, but relocating to the other side of the continent still seemed like a drastic step.

Ray couldn't stand the thought of his baby girl moving so far away from home. He was ready to simply refuse to let her go.

"We can't do that!" I told him. "She's twenty-three years old and a college graduate. She has to live her own life and make her own choices. She's made up her mind. If we tell her she can't go, she's going to resent us for trying to interfere and she'll go anyway. I think we have to support her decision. Our relationship to our daughter is too important not to."

Ray wasn't yet convinced. "She'll be 3,000 miles away. Who's going to be there when she needs help? We have no family out there. She doesn't know a single person in Southern California."

"You're right about that," I admitted, "which is why I need to go to California with her—to help her get settled."

I think Ray wondered whether Ros and I were *both* crazy at that point. However, while he certainly wasn't thrilled about the idea, he went along with it.

Ros and I flew into San Diego one afternoon and began the scenic drive up the coast toward Los Angeles, not yet sure of a destination. We rented a motel room in Huntington Beach—a town just southeast of LA—the first night. Ros was taken with the town and decided to look for housing there. The very next day she found a furnished studio apartment she liked in a complex with a security gate and guard (which I liked). The application and credit check took a couple days to process, so we used that time to scout the area and begin planning the best strategy for a job search.

"I'm willing to give it four weeks," I told her. "If you don't have a job by then, I think you need to think about coming back to North Carolina with me."

She didn't want to return home in defeat, so we got up early every day, grabbed a quick bite to eat, and then checked out the classifieds in the morning papers, marking every possibility that sounded interesting. We spent the rest of the day making calls, setting up appointments, picking up applications, and visiting companies for job interviews. We usually ate just one real meal a day (supper), after which Ros would work until bedtime filling out application forms while I scoured the "job opportunity" section in the evening papers and plotted whom to call and where to go the next day.

Fondly recalling those days recently, Ros laughed and accused me of being a real slave driver. She said she'd never worked harder in her life than she did looking for a job with me in California.

We never had to face my four-week deadline, fortunately. Ros landed a job with Security Pacific Bank the second week. I stayed a few days longer—just time enough to help her get a feel for the area, start making acquaintances at work, and begin to find a church family where she could eventually establish strong ties and build a caring support system. Then I went back home, still concerned that my daughter was living so far from home but confident that I'd done all I could by *being there* for her and with her during the transition and grateful that we would always share the memories of this adventure together.

My parenting experience has convinced me that the importance of *being there* for my children is magnified whenever they go through major transitions at any age—from those precious moments of bonding the first time you hold them after birth, to that first day of school, and for the rest of their lives.

Larry lived at home with Ray and me for a while after college. When it came time for him to move out, even though he was hoping to live just across town I went with him to help look for apartments. When Sis got married, Ray and I helped her and her husband buy and furnish their home. And when Ronnie and his wife, Blanca, who were both on active military service when they had their first baby girl, were assigned to simultaneous field duty, I volunteered my skills as grandmother to care for Nickie over several months.

Again, these weren't things we ever really thought twice about. They were all just a natural outgrowth of the ongoing desire Ray and I always had to *be there* for our children.

I won't pretend it was always easy. The cost was sometimes high — not just financially but emotionally as well.

There were lots of times when, if I'd had my preference, I would have enjoyed doing something besides traveling to yet another ballgame, sitting through one more PTA meeting, driving still another carpool stint, or fixing one more afternoon snack in my kitchen while waiting for the school bus. And yet, looking back, I don't regret one minute of it.

Sure, it took commitment and effort and sometimes sacrifice to *be there* for our children. But I don't hesitate to preach the importance of *being there* to any parents who will listen, because I've seen how crucial that presence was in my family. And you know, in all my talks to and discussions with other parents, I've never had anyone ever tell me, "I wish I'd spent more time at the office and less time with my children."

My work with the Michael Jordan Foundation has given me some firsthand exposure to the sad and troubled state of our society today. Millions of children regularly experience devastating violence, poverty, neglect, and abuse. It's a frightening world in which we're raising today's children. It's a tough time to be a parent.

None of us is ever fully prepared for the challenge of parenthood. From the time our children are born and for the rest of our lives, we find ourselves repeatedly surprised by the awesome responsibilities of the task we've been given. Any day, at any age, we can feel so inadequate that we look at our children, then at ourselves, and wonder, *Where do I start?*

I think you start by *being there*.

The year was 1957.

I knew the moment James Ronald Jordan was first placed in my arms that my life would never be the same again. Even as young as Ray and I were, we both sensed the significance of the occasion. The birth of our little baby boy had suddenly transformed our identities; we were now parents. And from that day on we would *always* be parents.

While we were too inexperienced to understand all the implications of our new identities, we understood this: our lives had been forever changed by Ronnie's birth. But the changes had just begun.

What we couldn't possibly imagine amidst our excitement—indeed, what few first-time parents realize—was that the birth of our precious oldest child was not the beginning just of *his* new little life. No, Ronnie's birth was also the beginning of a new life for Ray and for me—a life of constant, challenging change and sometimes painful adjustment.

Almost before we knew it, the year was 1974.

On a warm Friday night in May, Ray and I stood among an audience of parents, families, and friends in the auditorium at New Hanover High School. When our son's name was called—"James Ronald Jordan"—we watched proudly as a handsome young man strode purposefully across the platform to receive his diploma. I cried tears of joy and gratitude for my son that evening.

The next day we helped him finish packing. Then on Sunday I stood in a much smaller crowd—with Ray and our four younger children—at the Wilmington bus station to watch him walk confidently onto a bus headed for basic training at Fort Knox—the first step in his pursuit of a longtime dream of a career in the U.S. Army. I realized that once again my life had been changed forever. I wept tears of heart-wrenching grief as I waved goodbye and watched Ronnie's bus slowly disappear in the distance. I guess the rest of the family took their cue from me, because the kids and I all cried most of the way back home. Ray tried to console us (and himself) by saying, "He'll be fine. Don't worry: he'll be fine."

I could only go through the motions at work the next day. Fortunately, one of my roles at the bank was vault custodian. That meant I kept tabs on all the money going in and out of our branch's vault so that I could tally and oversee our daily shipments to the Federal Reserve Bank. It also meant I had a very private refuge I could flee to that day, whenever I felt myself about to burst into tears again.

I don't know how many times I disappeared into the quiet solitude of that vault that Monday before my supervisor came

Roslyn, Michael, senior and graduation photos from Laney High School

Larry, Delois, senior and graduation photos from Laney High School

Ronnie's 12th grade photo from New Hanover High School

in to make sure I was going to be all right. When I confessed the reason for my emotional state, he smiled sympathetically and told me to take all the time I needed. But for those next few difficult days, I wasn't sure there would be enough time in all of eternity to adjust to this new change, this agonizing sense of loss I felt.

Change.

When I think about my own experience as a mother, I can't help thinking of that word. Change is a constant at every stage of parenthood. It presents the primary challenge we face as parents. Indeed, it practically defines the job.

Change.

How well we deal with it and how well we do it goes a long way in determining our success or failure as parents.

In any discussion or rating of stress levels in various occupations, those tasks marked by high unpredictability and constant change are usually considered high-stress tasks. Is it any wonder, then, that so many of us feel stressed out by the responsibilities of parenthood? Is there anything more unpredictable or more constantly changing than children?

So how do we cope with the constant changes that occur from the time our children arrive in our homes until they leave and establish homes of their own?

For me, flexibility was key. To survive and succeed as a parent, I had to be willing and able to change and adapt, because parenting is all too often a trial-and-error experience.

There's no adequate preparation for parenthood, because there's no comparable experience. The most helpful and truly worthwhile training (perhaps the *only* helpful and worthwhile training) parents get is the on-the-job variety.

The humbling, frustrating truth is that as much as you eventually learn by experience, you can never completely master parenthood, because the job description keeps changing. About the time you feel pretty proficient in handling a newborn infant, he becomes a toddler. Just when you've survived the terrible twos and think you've learned to cope with a toddler, she's a preschooler. You get the preschool years almost figured out and it's time to begin kindergarten. Before you can get the early elementary years mastered, your son is a preadolescent sixth-grader. In no time your daughter is a teenager, and no one I know even pretends to be an expert at parenting teenagers. Suddenly it's time for your son to leave home, and you find yourself thinking, *If only I could start over knowing what I know now, parenting would be so much easier.*

The trouble with that idea (as any parent with more than one child knows) is that what you learn from your parenting experience with your first child has only limited application to your next one. No matter how many children you have, while there may be a few shared traits, each child is unique. What holds true of one, what works for one, may not hold true or work for the next one.

I certainly found that true in my family.

Ronnie was in many ways a typical first-born child. He was a pleaser. All of his life he has been a structured, responsible, reliable, determined, take-charge kind of person. Those personality traits make him an ideal military man. They're also the reason his adult siblings laughingly and respectfully call him by the nickname "Chief."

Delois (or "Sis," as the family calls her) was always at least as determined as her older brother when they were children. But perhaps because she was the first and only girl on the Jordan side of the family for some time (and was admittedly spoiled a bit in her younger days), Sis always seemed to want to do things her way. Furthermore, she always had very creative and definite ideas about how things needed to be. She had her own mind from the start, and she usually had that mind made up.

Larry had a much quieter intensity than Sis. A self-motivated, self-disciplined perfectionist, he would retreat to his room to pursue his own interests for hours or even days at a time. His personality was neither open nor demonstrative. He demanded so little attention that I had to make a deliberate attempt to interact with him on a regular basis.

Michael's personality seemed a real contrast to that of his easy-going older brother. While not as athletically gifted as Larry, Michael had an incredibly competitive nature and superior strength and size (he's now nearly a foot taller than either of his big brothers), which enabled him to compensate for the age difference. His affectionate and outgoing personality demanded a lot of attention within the family and beyond.

Roslyn was at once her own person and an interesting combination of all her older siblings. Like Ronnie, she was reliable, ambitious, and eager to please. Like Sis, she was creative and always knew her own mind. Like Larry, she seemed laid-back, quiet, and undemanding of her parents' attention.

Yet like Michael, she could be supercompetitive, determined to excel at whatever she did.

Five kids. Five very different personalities. Five different places in one family. Five different relationships with their mother and father, and a multitude of different relationships one to another. Mix these kids together, factor in their different ages and varying rates of development, and you get such a dynamic, ever-changing, and complex pattern of interpersonal, interlocking, intrafamily relationships that it becomes clearly impossible to have the exact same relationship with all five children at once.

Not that you love any one of them any more or less than the rest. And not that you have different goals or utilize different parenting principles. But your specific strategy for implementing your principles and the exact route you take in pursuit of your goals may vary considerably in response to the different personalities and needs of your very different children.

Here's where I think having a large family actually proved advantageous to us. In this day and age, when so many parents choose to limit their families to just two children, it's easy for folks to expect both kids to fit pretty much the same personality mold and have the same basic needs. Then, in a well-meaning but misguided attempt to be fair and equitable, they compound the problem by trying to treat them and relate to them in exactly the same way.

When you have five kids, one of them is (or all five of them are) always out of sync with siblings. Experience quickly forces you to recognize the folly of expecting them to think, act, respond, or relate in the same way. If you're going to survive with any semblance of sanity, you have to constantly tailor your parenting to fit the needs of your very different children.

While that may sound simple and natural in theory, putting the theory into practice can be a real trick.

I've heard people compare parenthood to a juggling act, and I suppose it is. But not just the simple three-tennis-balls-in-the-air trick. When I think of parents as jugglers, I picture a blindfolded performer handling five different objects at once—perhaps a roaring chainsaw, a flaming torch, a priceless antique crystal goblet, a lace handkerchief, and a robin's egg—each requiring a careful but varied grip.

Not only may the differing personalities of one or more children require very different handling, but various circumstances and ages dictate further adjustments. You can't protect, teach, discipline, or motivate any one child the same way, in every situation, all of his or her life. Indeed, I've found that one of the greatest challenges of parenthood is knowing just how to change your handling technique and when to alter your grip.

The challenge grows more and more difficult with age. We naturally and easily hold a newborn tight and close. And that's good, because babies need our protection and warmth. Being held often and snugly gives them a sense of security, well-being, and trust that is essential to the development of a healthy personality.

Fortunately, holding our babies tight is instinctive. Even the most inexperienced and awkward new father learns this essential skill quickly.

Unfortunately, an equally important skill needed to raise emotionally healthy and independent individuals—knowing how and when to loosen the grip—is not at all instinctive. In fact, it goes against the grain of our natural protective tendency. For most parents, the art of letting go takes a lifetime to learn.

God in his infinite wisdom ordained nine months as the proper and necessary time period for all the incredible, miraculous changes that take place in a woman's body as she prepares to bring a healthy new baby into this world. For most pregnant women, those nine months of anticipation and preparation seem plenty long enough. By the time that due date arrives, they're physically and emotionally ready to give birth.

So how is it, if nine months often seems too long to wait to bring a child into our family, that eighteen years seldom seems long enough to prepare to send them out into the world? For those of you who haven't yet experienced this for yourselves, let me offer a warning you may not want to hear: in my experience, the ordeal of birth is nothing compared to the agony of letting go.

It's undoubtedly the biggest, most difficult adjustment parents have to make, but we can't escape it. Sooner if not later, we're going to have to do it.

The reminders are everywhere and frequent. They come every time some relative at a family reunion exclaims, "That child is growing like a weed!" Every time we measure a son's height against the kitchen doorframe. Every time a daughter wants to stand back-to-back with her mother, asking "Who's taller now?"

As much as we enjoy our children's excitement about growing, there's a bit of sadness involved for most parents. That's because there's usually a part of us that doesn't want to let go.

Yet children are so anxious to grow up. At least all mine were—especially Michael.

He was always a big kid compared to my other children. He caught up to and passed his older brother Larry in height by the time he started school. But he always wanted to be taller yet—so he could compete at sports with the older boys in the neighborhood and so he could jump like his hero, David Thompson, who played basketball for North Carolina State.

I can't count the number of times he said to me, "Mama, I want to be taller."

I used to laugh and tell him, "When you go to bed tonight, Mama will pray over you and put salt in your shoes to help you grow!"

"Will I be taller in the morning then?" he would ask. "How much?"

"Maybe a little bit," I told him. "We'll have to wait and see how much."

I don't remember why I ever said I'd have to put salt in his shoes. It was just something silly I thought up, and then it became part of our regular routine. I never actually put salt in his shoes, but I did pray.

So did Michael. He went through a stage when he prayed every night at bedtime that the Lord would make him taller.

When our prayers were finally answered and he began to shoot up as a young teenager, people would comment on how fast he was growing. And Michael would often tell them it was because his mother put salt in his shoes and prayed over him every night. Eventually I had to tell him the truth: that I'd never put salt in his shoes but had just prayed.

Whatever the explanation, it seemed to work. Michael grew so fast, going from 5'7" to 6'0" his sophomore year in high school, that he literally experienced growing pains. He'd wake up in the morning with his knees hurting so bad he wasn't sure he could go to school. When I took him to the orthopedist, the doctor said the problem was that the bones in his legs were growing so fast that they were creating a gap in his knee joints. He prescribed aspirin and warned Michael he would have to get used to the pain, explaining that the X rays he'd taken indicated that Michael had several more inches to grow. The man's prediction proved to be right: Michael's knees didn't finally quit hurting until he was in college. By then he was 6'4" and well on the way to his current height of 6'6", which he reached after a couple of years in the NBA.

But I still had a few lessons to learn about letting go.

For me, one of the hardest parts of loosening the grip was allowing my teenage and young-adult children to pursue their own dreams, make life-impacting decisions, and choose paths that wouldn't have been my first option for them. I struggled in this regard with each of my children.

Ronnie was the kind of kid who lined his shoes up straight in the bottom of his closet and always wanted the crease on his dress pants ironed a certain way. I guess it shouldn't have been too surprising when he announced, at the age of thirteen or fourteen, that he'd decided he would be an "Army man" when he grew up, though I thought his personality would be just as ideally suited to engineering or some similar career. Even after he joined the Junior ROTC in high school and began to work his way up the ranks of leadership, I secretly hoped he'd soon get his fill of things military. But he didn't.

When we finally realized just how serious he was about a military career, we raised the possibility of participating in college ROTC and then going into the service as an officer. Ronnie didn't want to wait, however. He enlisted early and shipped out for boot camp two days after his high school graduation.

We had to let go. And we did. We even tried to affirm his decision by being there, proud and supportive, at the graduation ceremonies after his basic and advanced training.

As the older daughter, Delois was even harder for Ray and me to let go. It worried me when she was in high school that so many of her friends dreamed only of getting married and starting a family as soon as possible. A couple of them even dropped out of school to have babies.

I wanted more for Sis. When she began to get serious with her boyfriend, I resorted to my own mother's failed strategy.

We sent Sis off in the summers to visit relatives in Philadelphia in hopes that our artistically gifted and creative daughter might discover the excitement of the big wide world and see the value of getting a little more exposure and experience before settling down to raise a family in Wilmington.

We planned to insist that she try college. But after visiting King's College of Design in Raleigh to check out their design program, my strong-willed daughter told us she had made up her mind: marriage over education. Unwilling to fight a hopeless battle and risk losing our relationship with Sis in the process, we used the money we'd set aside for her education to give her a wedding and help the newlyweds get a small place of their own. Once again I was forced to loosen my grip, let go, and allow my child to go her own way.

Larry presented a very different problem. He was such a quiet, reserved homebody that there were a number of years when Ray and I wondered if he'd ever leave home to establish a life and family of his own. Loosening the grip and letting him go was no problem; *getting* him to go was something else. Both Michael and Ros had been on their own for some time when Larry and I went apartment hunting. I wanted to make sure he found something. But I also wanted to assure him that our letting go didn't mean the end of our caring or our relationship.

When Michael began considering the option of turning pro after his junior year at Carolina, I opposed the idea. Even when Ray and Coach Smith agreed that it made sense for him to go into the NBA draft, I wanted him to stay and graduate. But Michael took me aside and assured me that a pro basketball career wouldn't keep him from getting his college degree. He promised he would come back in the off-season to finish up the required coursework—not just because I wanted him to but because a college degree was important to him as well. When I heard that, I knew the time had come for me to let go and allow Michael to pursue his dream.

I'd actually come to that point with Ros three years earlier when she announced that she wanted to go off to college after her junior year of high school. I worried that she was too young to start college at sixteen, but I was even more troubled by what seemed an almost desperate determination to leave home. I hadn't thought she was so unhappy that she couldn't wait to get out from under our roof.

Michael finally pulled me aside one day and enlightened me. It seems he and Larry had been teasing Ros for some time by reminding her that she was the "baby" of the family and speculating about how spoiled her life was going to be as the only child still at home once Michael and Larry were both away at school.

She'd taken such offense at her brothers' calling her the baby of the family that she vowed she wouldn't be left behind by herself. When Michael left for college, she was going to leave home too.

Once I understood the reasons and had checked with her teachers and counselors to make sure they felt she was prepared, I was finally ready to let go and encourage Ros to follow the course she had set for herself.

I won't try to tell you it was easy to loosen the grip and let go. I can't even say it got easier as each child left home.

The truth is the empty-nest syndrome was the hardest thing Ray and I ever had to face together. We felt lost. In some ways we had to begin our relationship all over again: we had to find out who we were, discover new things to talk about, and learn how to relate to each other apart from our kids.

It wasn't so much that we were unhappy with each other as it was that our children had always been such a huge source of happiness in our lives that we desperately missed the familiar, everyday role of parents we'd enjoyed for all our adult lives. For a couple years after the kids left home, whenever Ray read a newspaper story about an abandoned child or saw a clip about refugee children on television he would raise the possibility of beginning a new adoptive family. And he was serious. I told him, though, that we were both too old to start over and that I'd rather learn to enjoy grandparenthood.

So what's the secret for surviving all the changes and making all the adjustments required by childhood and parenthood? Isn't there more to be said than simply "Parents need to be flexible"?

Though I've discovered no magic formula, I've learned that the ever-changing roles and challenges of parenthood seem a lot easier once people adopt a changing vision of parenthood—at least that's been my experience. I find that it helps to think of parenthood as a series of stages determined by the needs of our children and the kind of relationship they need with us at different points in their lives.

Let me explain. Babies and young children need their parents to be mothers and fathers. They need someone to lead and protect them, care for their basic needs, offer them security and comfort, provide limits, and discipline and correct them. In short, young children need their parents to be mamas and daddies.

As children get older, as they approach and enter adolescence, their needs and our roles as parents change. I found it helpful at that stage to think of myself less as a mama and more as a teacher. While adolescents still need a lot of the same things they needed as young children, they're ready for more information and reasoning. They want opportunities to experience and learn; they need assignments to complete, skills to master. They need guidance and direction. All these things come more naturally when we view our role more as that of a teacher than that of a mother or father.

At some point, maybe when the kids are in college or early adulthood, the primary role of a parent changes yet again—from that of teacher to that of friend. Unfortunately, not enough parents ever embrace this vision of parenthood. Many of those who do—those who manage to complete the often tricky transformation from parent as mother/father, to parent as teacher, and finally to parent as friend—will testify that this last stage of parenthood can be the most satisfying and rewarding of all.

Let me make some things very clear here. In dividing my vision of parenthood into these three stages, I don't want to be too simplistic. I don't see these divisions as rigid or think that the roles are exclusive and distinct. I'm certainly not saying that when a child turns twelve, his parents need to quit being mama or daddy to become teacher; neither am I saying that after a child's twenty-first birthday a parent can no longer be any more than her friend.

As long as I live, I'll always be the mama of my five children, and they all know that. They'll never be so old that they won't sometimes need their mother's protection, comfort, and correction; and I won't hesitate to give those things when I can. Neither will they ever be so old that they can't benefit from the guidance of my words and actions; I hope I haven't stopped being a teacher to them.

But I find great comfort and guidance in my ongoing relationship with my adult children when I remind myself that my *primary* role as their parent today is to be their friend. Not just any friend, but a unique, lifelong friend who understands them and loves them like no one else in the world.

My new vision of parenthood as friendship sometimes limits what I do or say. But that's not necessarily bad. Asking myself, "What would a friend do or say in this situation?" can serve to rein me in, to stop me before I complicate or damage my relationship by instinctively charging into a situation as a teacher or a mama.

I still make mistakes. I have to admit that I too often stick my mama's nose in where a sensitive friend would back off. I sometimes lecture like a teacher when a wise friend would keep quiet and listen.

However, I have no doubt that I'd make a lot more mistakes if I didn't understand this concept of a changing vision of parenthood. Putting it into practice, like so much of parenting, is a trial-and-error experience. But this concept has helped me adjust to and cope with the constantly changing demands of being a parent.

It has also helped me appreciate the rewards that come with the job. I always enjoyed being a mama—looking into my baby's eyes and feeling needed. I found great satisfaction in watching my children grow and realizing how quickly and well they were learning the important lessons I worked so hard to teach them.

But I can honestly say that nothing I ever experienced in those early stages of parenthood seemed any sweeter than the satisfaction I feel today when Ronnie calls to ask my advice on dealing with a woman who works for him. When Sis needs encouragement to deal with her own two strong-willed teenagers. When Michael and I discuss plans and dreams for the foundation. When Larry wants to talk about his role as a husband and father and asks me to talk about relevant experiences Ray and I shared. Or when Ros calls and invites me to join her on her church's mission trip to Jamaica because she thinks I'd enjoy the experience and she hasn't spent enough time with me lately.

Being a friend to your adult children can be a terrific experience. It's a worthy goal for all parents, and it's one of parenthood's greatest rewards.

But you have to be willing and able to change. You have to be flexible. You have to learn to gradually loosen the grip, remembering that change can be good.

5

As mothers, we carry babies in our bodies for nine long, difficult months. We give birth to those babies in what's one of the
most physically taxing experiences of our lives. We schedule
our entire days so we can nurse or feed our children during
those first months of their lives. And even those of us who
have involved, caring, helpful husbands change the vast majority of the babies' diapers ourselves. So it hardly seems fair
that the very first intelligible word most babies utter is *da-da*.

I know it was the first thing any of my five children said.
And I can still picture the look of sheer joy and pride that
word brought to their father's face. Ray would exclaim, "Did
you hear that, honey? He called me Da-da!" Or "Would you
listen to that! This baby knows her daddy!" Pretending not to
believe him, I'd say, "Let's see if she'll say it again with both of
us listening."

Whether the baby is the first child or the fifteenth, I think
every mother experiences an unforgettable thrill when her in-

fant babbles his or her first unmistakable syllables—even when the word is *da-da*. And you certainly never forget the overwhelming tidal wave of warmth that rolls over you the first morning you hear the sweetest sound in the world—the two glorious syllables *ma-ma*—as those little arms reach up from the crib.

We hear and remember those initial words as important milestones in a child's development because we know that words are the building blocks of communication and that communication forms the foundation of all human relationships.

Before you know it, that sprinkling of simple baby sounds becomes a torrent of words conveying information and emotion. Anytime I stop to remember, I can still hear the echo of excitement that filled the house the moment the kids burst through the door after school: "Mama! We got our report cards today, and I got an A in English! Can you believe it?" Or "Mama, Mama! Guess what! I made the cheerleading team! I wasn't sure I would, but I did. I feel so happy!"

But the communication doesn't always flow so freely. There are times when getting information out of your children is like pulling teeth. You ask what happened at school, and you get that favorite adolescent response: "Oh, nothing."

Fortunately, a lot of parents quickly discover that there's more to communication than words. We learn to listen between the lines, to find insight in what's *not* said, to detect the unspoken by the choice or words or the inflection of voice.

Many moms seem to have a built-in truth detector. I know my children thought I did. They laughingly tell me today, "You had a way of looking at us as if you knew the score. And we *knew* you knew, so we couldn't lie."

They're right. I often did know. And when I wasn't sure, I could usually manage to look at them as if I were. Pretty quickly they'd drop their little heads in resignation and admit the truth.

The older kids get, the harder it is to fool them into think-ing you always know the truth. And yet the older they get—at least in the case of my children—the better parents know them and the easier it is for parents to pick up on unspoken clues that reveal what kids are feeling and thinking.

After Delois left home to get married and start her family, we'd regularly talk on the phone. I could usually tell just by the tone of her voice what kind of day she was having. Sis was always such a determined, independent person that when she was feeling particularly discouraged or stressed, she seldom came right out and admitted it. But I could tell just by how she sounded when I needed to keep her talking long enough to open up or when I needed to jump in the car and head over to her house to see what I could do to help.

Communication.

In anybody's book, it's key to parenting. In my way of thinking, it's every bit as important to parents' survival and success as being there for the kids or being flexible.

I realize countless books have been written on the sub-ject, and lots of people make their living trying to help people improve their communication skills. I'm afraid I can't offer any startling new insights into communication theory. Not even any revolutionary advice on how parents can better relate to kids.

What my experience has taught me is the absolute importance of a few basic lessons. These lessons are things most parents know or have heard somewhere, but we all need to be reminded of them at one time or another.

One of the most crucial of those lessons is that good communication doesn't happen in a vacuum. It requires a real-life setting. In other words, parents who want good communication in their families have to provide a place and time for that communication to occur.

The single biggest reason so many families don't enjoy good communication seems painfully obvious to me: they seldom have the opportunity. They simply never find the time to communicate, because they're together so infrequently.

Family meals were the foundation of communication in the Jordan home. We saw dinnertime not just as the source of necessary nutrition but as a chance to keep in touch with each other's lives, maintain family ties, and nurture relationships by communicating with each other.

I'm not going to try to tell you that the conversation was always scintillating and meaningful. Indeed, with five children, there were more than enough spills, interruptions, and outbreaks of bickering to make mealtimes lively (if not chaotic).

But as each person shared details about his or her day, as we heard the good and the bad that had happened, as we laughed and told stories about the things we'd seen and the people we'd encountered, we were establishing a daily pattern of sharing. We were developing a habit of talking together about anything and everything. And Ray and I were constantly on the lookout for comments, subjects of concern, even attitudes and feelings that might crop up at the table—things we thought we probably ought to discuss ourselves or topics we thought might require a little deeper digging and discussion with the kids at a later time or in a different setting.

Family trips and vacations offered the Jordan family similar opportunities for communication. When you're crowded in a car for eight straight hours, or when you spend twenty-four hours a day with each other for a week away from home, you're forced to communicate in ways that just don't happen in the daily routine at home.

So even after our children became teenagers, had their own friends and interests, and began to sometimes feel that it wasn't cool to go places with their parents and siblings, we insisted on family trips and vacations. Such trips seemed essential to us because they provided a natural atmosphere of togetherness and communication. If one of the kids expressed a reluctance to go—say, Roslyn wasn't excited about another trip across the state for her brothers' baseball tournament—we'd sometimes suggest that she invite a friend along to make the prospect of family time more appealing.

We knew, of course, that good communication in our family required more than routine group time around the table or on the road somewhere. We also needed to have regular, meaningful, one-on-one interaction with each of our children. When you have five children, just finding the time for such interaction can be a major challenge. It demands deliberate effort and more than a little planning.

Here's where I found the kind of flexibility I talked about in Chapter 4 so important. Because all of my children were different, they often required different approaches when it came to one-on-one communication.

The kids' openness to various forms of communication varied not only from person to person but also at different stages of their lives (and sometimes from day to day). As a rule, though, Ronnie found it a little easier to open up with me, while Sis related more comfortably to Ray. Then Larry came along, and it often took both Ray and me to draw him out. Michael was always such an open person, his feelings so close to the surface, that with very little prodding he'd usually talk to whichever one of us was there. Ros, our next child, was perhaps more like Larry: we had to make sure we drew her out. Sometimes she found it easier to talk to her daddy; at other times she'd open up to me.

Ray and I learned that it took both of us to have good communication with all five of our kids. And to pull that unified approach off, we had to communicate well with each other. This was in part because we needed to share our insights before deciding what to say. But it was also because we wanted to make certain we were both on the same page; we always thought it critical that we agree on what and how we communicated to our kids. If parents don't communicate with each other, it's too easy for them to get manipulated.

I learned to be wary whenever one of the kids walked into the kitchen, gave me a hug, and said something like, "Hey, Mom! Dad said I could use the car tonight as long as it's okay with you."

I could usually read the disappointment in the kids' eyes when I responded (as I generally did), "He did, did he? Well, let me talk to him, and we'll let you know what we decide."

In talking to Ray, I often discovered that what he'd really said was something like, "If you're willing to do such and such, we'll think about it, as long as it's okay with your mother."

By the time the request came to me, however, any conditions Ray might have imposed had been conveniently left out; the request was generally presented in such a way as to make it seem as if all I needed to do was rubber-stamp Ray's decision. We quickly learned that to avoid being manipulated and to survive with our own relationship intact, we had to counter our kids' divide-and-conquer strategy by talking to each other.

That's not to say Ray and I always saw eye to eye on child-rearing strategies or on what we should tell our kids in a given situation. Sometimes I went along with what he felt best, at other times we followed my instincts, and much of the time we took a compromise position. But by talking and reaching agreement together, Ray and I usually managed to present a strong and united front to our children. That kind of communication between parents makes a huge difference in how well we as parents communicate with our kids.

What are we communicating to our children? Most of us who are parents would do well to ask ourselves that question often and try to answer it honestly. After all, what we say is as important as when and how we say it.

A lot of the communication parents have with children involves the simple transfer of information and the relaying of instructions. As crucial as it is for family members to share the details of each other's lives, to know who's doing what, where, and when, an awful lot of families don't manage very well even at this most basic level of communication. And too many of those who do don't realize that good communication requires much more.

In addition to information and instruction, we as parents need to communicate our interest and concern to our children. How do we do that? I think we make a good start when we stop talking and make a concerted effort to listen to what our kids are saying (and refraining from saying). It's so easy to concentrate our attention on what *we* want to say, what *we* know they need to hear, that we don't sit back and listen for what *they* need to talk about.

We miss the boat when we forget that the most effective communication is two-way communication. That sometimes the best means of conveying our interest and concern is to let our kids set the agenda before we respond. That we should often take our cue from our kids in deciding what to talk about. That we need to be able and willing to discuss anything, letting our kids know no subject is too big or too small.

But good communication, *meaningful* communication, demands even more. We must not only frequently get beneath the surface of information transfer but also penetrate below the intermediate level of conveying interest and concern: we need to expose and honestly express our deepest feelings.

Not that children need to know, or even *should* know, all that their parents are struggling with. I've seen too many families in which parents have dumped their own personal problems—professional, financial, even marital—on children who weren't emotionally equipped or mature enough to handle the load. Indeed, this sort of spill-all communication is one of the most common ways kids are being forced into adulthood prematurely today. It's wrong, and it's harmful. Instead, we as parents need to shield our children from things they just aren't yet ready to communicate about.

For example, like most couples who've been married for years—for us, it was more than thirty years at the time of Ray's death—Ray and I experienced our ups and downs. But when we had our differences, we tried to keep them between the two of us so as not to upset or burden the kids. In talking to the kids now, as adults—especially in the context of open and honest discussion of various marriage- and family-related topics—I'll come out and say, "Your dad and I really had to work through this issue," or "I had to go to our minister for advice when that happened."

Invariably the kids will react with surprise and exclaim, "We didn't know that!" or "Why didn't you ever say anything about this before?"

And I'll tell them, "We didn't think you'd understand back then; you would've worried. You simply didn't need to know at the time. Now that you're an adult, we can talk about it. Maybe it will even help you to hear what we went through and what lessons we learned."

One of the emotions that's always appropriate and essential to communicate to our children is love. When we don't know what to say, we can seldom go wrong by asking ourselves, *How can I communicate my love in this situation?* We're going to talk about the important tool of unconditional love in the next chapter, but I need to mention it here as well, in the discussion of communication, because love is one of the most important things we must communicate to our children.

Along with love we need to communicate encouragement—something I think too many parents fail to understand. Later in this book, we're going to talk about the importance of encouraging children to dream and set goals. I see this as one of the most influential things parents can do for their children.

There's so much positive power in encouragement—especially parental encouragement. On the flip side, there's such devastating power in negative words of criticism and judgment that even one negative word may require many positive ones to balance it out in a son's or daughter's mind. We need to weigh our words carefully and err, if we're going to err, on the positive, uplifting side of encouragement. Our children will bless us for it one day if we do.

At the beginning of this book I talked about the demand for *commitment* in parenting. Nowhere is that commitment more needed than in this area of communication. I've discovered that good communication requires time, energy, diligence, sensitivity, and a lot of hard work. In the process of that discovery, I've found a handful of practical guidelines I'd like to share with you.

First, *when you don't know what to communicate or how to relate to something one of your sons or daughters is going through, think back to your own childhood.* I know lots of things have changed; kids today face situations and problems I couldn't have imagined when I was a girl. And yet, while today's settings and circumstances often seem unfamiliar to me, the basic range of human emotion remains the same. What scares kids today may be very different from the things that scared me as a child, but fear itself hasn't changed all that much. I may not have experienced the same kind of abusive language my children heard when they were at school, but I remember the embarrassment and pain I felt when I was young and people called me fat. So even when we can't always identify with the situations kids live in today, we can relate to the basic emotions they feel. And we can start to communicate there.

Second, *choose your words carefully. Be positive and encouraging, but also be clear in what you communicate.* Sometimes I don't say what I mean, and other times I don't really mean what I say. Yet as a parent I can't afford to be too big to admit to myself and to my children when I've made a mistake. Likewise, if anger or some other emotion makes me say something I regret, I need to apologize and clarify what I should have said. And when I misspeak myself for any reason, I can't be too proud to go back and explain, "What I really meant was . . ." or "What I should have said is that . . ."

Third, *one-sided communication is a lot better than no communication at all.* There were times (and not only when the kids were going through adolescence) when my children were unwilling or unable to open up and say much about some subject I thought important enough to discuss. I learned to say what I thought needed to be said, to anticipate the unspoken feelings, and to respond to the unvoiced questions. And while I wasn't always sure how effective my one-sided communication was at the time, I took comfort in doing what I could to keep communication channels open for future use.

Fourth, *repetition may get old—for parents as well as kids—but it works.* I'm one of those mothers who operated under the assumption that if something was important enough to say once, it needed to be said again and again. Many is the time one of my children would say, "Mama, you told me that. You don't have to say it again."

I took real satisfaction one day recently when Sis called to talk about some of the things she'd been going through with her teenagers, Cory and Sherri. "I find myself repeating something the same way you did, Mother. But I get tired of telling the kids the same thing over and over again." I had to laugh as I told her, "Now you know what I went through with you. But you can't stop saying it. No matter how many times it takes, you've got to keep saying it and saying it until it's in their heads, until you know they understand what you're saying and they won't ever be able to forget."

"But it's so hard," Sis lamented.

"I know," I agreed, laughing again.

Fifth, *when everything is said and done, just pray.* I did my best to communicate with my children. Then I communicated with God. I prayed every day that he would help my sons understand, that he would help my daughters understand, and that someday my children would appreciate my commitment to communication and love me all the more for it.

I've made so much of the effort involved in communication that I need to balance that with an encouraging word. Let me add that I firmly believe communication efforts eventually pay off.

Perhaps the greatest rewards of good communication begin about the time our primary role as parents shifts from that of teacher to that of friend. With most of my kids, that transition took place somewhere around the end of their freshman year of college, after they'd been away from home and on their own for a while.

The rewards of communication really hit home for me when Ros was in college. When we were talking one day, she confided that she was concerned about a friend of hers with a drug problem. She knew that this friend needed help, but she didn't know what to do. I said, "You need to encourage him to talk to his parents and let them find him some professional help."

"I did," Ros said, "but he doesn't think he could ever talk to his parents about something like this."

"Then maybe you could encourage him to go to a counselor or the campus minister. Maybe such a person could contact the parents and begin to get him the help he needs."

It saddened me to think about this family's lack of communication, but at the same time I was heartened that Roslyn felt free to share her own concern with me—not as a mother who might warn her about being friends with someone who used drugs, not as a teacher who would lecture her, but as a friend who could empathize and share her uncertainty about what she might do to help.

I'm convinced that it's our family's commitment to communication, more than any other factor, that enables me to say today that my five children are the best friends I have in the world. A lifetime of practice and effort has made communication a wonderful and rewarding habit for us.

No matter what I'm doing, no matter where in the world I am, I talk to one or more of my children every day—if not in person, at least by phone. I talk with my daughters the most, but hardly a week goes by that I don't talk to each of the kids. And it's gotten so even my boys call me as often as I phone them: Ronnie always lets me know when he's going out on a field assignment and won't be calling, and Michael and Larry make a special point of checking in with me anytime they haven't heard from me for a few days.

It's interesting what all you learn when you begin to communicate with your children as friends. I don't think we ever get together as a family anymore that I don't receive some revelation I'd never have suspected about my kids' childhood. It wasn't until recently that my sons laughingly described their adventures chasing Granddad's pigs. "He'd have skinned you alive if he'd caught you doing that!" I said, amazed.

And then there are the memories of mischief we *all* remember because we all shared in it. Like the way Grandma's famous biscuits had a habit of disappearing off the kitchen counter before she could get them to the dining room table. I can almost taste those biscuits whenever any of the kids talks about eating at their Grandmother Bell's house. No one—and I know, because I tried for years before I finally gave up—could ever make biscuits quite like Ray's mom. When they came hot out of the oven, the temptation to snitch one was too much for hungry grandchildren (and children) to resist.

Today we all remember and laugh about the way Grandma would fuss when she'd bring a half-empty bread plate to the table and we'd all pretend we knew nothing about the missing biscuits. Grandma enjoyed the little ritual too much to really get upset. And Ray and I couldn't say much to the kids, because we were usually as guilty as they were.

But as far as I'm concerned, the greatest result of our family communication strategy is neither the daily phone calls nor the times we spend now reminiscing and laughing about things that happened years ago. I find even greater satisfaction when I recognize some of Ray's words and my words being echoed by our children today.

It happens when I hear some of the things Sis tells her teenage children. It happens when Michael stands up in front of a group of kids and tells them that achieving their dreams is going to require commitment and a willingness to work hard. It happens when Roslyn makes a foundation presentation for the Michael Jordan Education Club and talks about the importance of learning, stressing that no one can ever take a person's education away.

Whenever I hear my own words and ideas being expressed by my adult children, it thrills my soul as a mother. I have to say, "Thank you, Lord. They really were listening. It didn't just go in one ear and out the other. We truly were *communicating.*"

CHAPTER

6

He didn't look sick. That was one reason I spotted him right away—that and the fact he followed our group everywhere we went in the hospital that afternoon.

I had come to deliver Christmas presents to the young patients in one of the hospitals our foundation supports. As I worked my way room by room through the children's wards, this active little guy always seemed to be in the thick of the action—holding a nurse's hand, getting tickled by one of the doctors, curiously eyeing all the brightly wrapped packages, and watching with eager anticipation as each gift was opened. No other child in the hospital seemed to get the attention or be allowed the freedom this boy did. He was so obviously a staff favorite that I naturally wondered why.

One of the administrators leading our tour answered my question. "Oh, that's . . . ," she said, whispering a name as if she expected me to know it. When she saw that the name didn't register with me, she added, "You probably remember his case from the news these last few weeks."

Then I remembered. His was a story so horrible that it had been picked up by the wire services and given national coverage. Police had arrested a drug-addicted mother and her boyfriend and had discovered the child, alone and hungry, locked in a dark closet in their apartment. What had shocked even the social workers on the case, and what had drawn media attention, was the eventual determination that this six-year-old boy had spent a major portion of his short life locked away in that tiny unlighted, unventilated closet. He hadn't gone to school. He hadn't played with, or even known, other children. He'd eaten only what scraps his mother had brought him—when she'd remembered to feed him. He'd seen the light of day only on those infrequent occasions when his mother had given him time out of his closet for good behavior.

"That's the boy I read about in the papers?" I couldn't believe it. "He seems so outgoing and cheerful!"

The administrator nodded and smiled. "Our hospital staff has spoiled him. The doctors and nurses give him pretty much free run of this wing. Knowing how he was abused all those years, no one has the heart to restrict him. He's really a sweet kid. You have to meet him."

"I'd like that," I replied.

The next time the youngster cruised past, introductions were made: "This is Mrs. Jordan, Michael Jordan's mother."

He gave me a big smile as I took his hand. "Do you know who Michael Jordan is?" I asked, figuring I'd need to explain.

He nodded. "The great basketball player."

"That's right!" I responded, marveling that even a child who'd spent much of his life locked in a dark closet would know of my son. As we chatted, I discovered that this was a bright and charming little guy. I couldn't help wondering how much sharper he would have been if he hadn't been so mistreated. I thought about the love I had for my children and tried in vain to imagine how any parent could have done what had been done to such a lovable little boy.

Relatively few children know the degree of abuse (or make the headlines) that this boy did. But I meet enough needy kids through the work of our foundation to know that there are thousands upon thousands of precious children in our country today who aren't getting the kind of love and care they need.

At virtually every school I visit, at least one child will approach me to ask, "Mrs. J., will you give me a hug?" And while I can't always take the time required to sign autographs or to pose with everyone who wants a photo taken with me, I usually make time to dispense hugs. I know how important love and affection are, and I see how hungry these kids are for such things.

Just how important is it to be and feel loved?

Ask any psychiatrist or counselor. They'll all tell you that love—being loved, feeling loved, and expressing love—is at issue with most of the people who come to them for help. The kind of love we experience as children greatly impacts both our self-confidence and our ability to achieve. It serves as a pattern—good or bad—for every relationship we have in life. It even affects our potential for faith and trust.

Love is every bit as important a human need as food, clothing, and shelter, because it's our early experience of love that in large part determines how we view and relate to ourselves, others, even God—for the rest of our lives.

So how can we as parents make sure our children get the love necessary to develop into happy, healthy human beings?

I think we have to start by first realizing, then constantly reminding ourselves, how important love is. Once we understand that importance, we can begin to see love as perhaps the most critical, powerful, and invaluable parenting tool we have at our disposal. How we wield it shapes our children forever.

I meet and talk with many parents in the course of our foundation's work with children and families. I can generally tell that they love their children. They say they do, and I believe them. I'm convinced it's only a very rare and very disturbed parent who doesn't or can't love his or her child.

But then why do I find so many kids who seem so desperately hungry for love?

I've come to the conclusion that it's not enough for us to love our children. Most of us do that. The bigger challenge is making sure they *feel* loved. We can love them more than life itself, but unless our children *sense* our love, they'll never experience the power and benefits love can make in a person's life.

And how do we make sure our children feel loved? I have no earth-shattering advice—just a couple simple principles we as parents need to be reminded of on a regular basis.

The first principle is obvious but crucial: express your love verbally. I tried to make sure my children knew that they were loved by telling them often—every day and at every possible opportunity.

I told them I loved them when I tucked them into bed at night. When I dropped them off at school in the morning. When they skinned their knees. When a friend hurt their feelings.

When I punished them, I explained that I did so because I loved them and wanted them to learn the right way to act. Kids sometimes have a hard time believing that love can be our motivation for correction, but that's all the more reason to keep saying it.

When I felt the need to shield the kids from something—for example, not letting them go somewhere they'd asked to go or do something they wanted to do—I'd tell them I was trying to protect them "because I love you."

When I stayed up at night until my teenagers came home, I told them it wasn't because I didn't trust them. "I worry because I love you so much."

When they complained about, or just rolled their eyes at, a repeat lecture from me, I'd remind them, "You know that the reason I'm saying this again is that I love you."

I think it's a good idea also to remind kids of the reason that you do things for them and with them. "Why are we taking family vacation time to drive halfway across the state to take you to this baseball tournament you're playing in?" Or "Why did I get up before dawn on a Saturday morning to help you pick up the doughnuts your Girl Scout troop is selling?"

Or "Why did I knock myself out to rearrange my afternoon so I could pick you up after cheerleading practice?" Not because there isn't anything I'd rather do. Not even because it's something expected of good parents. "I do it gladly because I love you."

Even today, I never have a phone conversation with any one of my five children that doesn't end the same way. Before we hang up, one of us will always say, "I love you," and the other will reply, "I love you too."

We can only hope that if we say it enough to our kids, the message will sink in. In the meantime, the repetition serves as a regular reminder for us parents as well. It can temper our words and our actions and help us keep our most important motivation in mind.

And yet no matter how often we tell our children we love them, they won't be convinced without further evidence. Our words will ring hollow if we don't back them up with our actions. It's not enough to *say*, "I love you." The second principle, then, is that our lives and our homes have to *demonstrate* our love. And we can ensure that they do so in two important ways.

The first way we demonstrate our love in action is with physical affection. That came easy and often in the Jordan household, because Ray and I both were naturally affectionate—with each other as well as with the children.

The first thing Ray did when he got home from work in the evening was to walk into the kitchen and reach for me; he'd give me a kiss or maybe lift me up off my feet in a big hug. He also had a habit of sneaking up behind me when I was doing dishes and making me jump by smacking me on my bottom. I'd snap, "Stop that!" and we'd both laugh.

I remember the afternoon when Mr. Michael, who was about twelve or thirteen, decided he'd sneak into the kitchen and pop Mama on the backside. When I jumped and exclaimed as usual, he began to laugh.

"Just what do you think you're doing!" I demanded. "You don't hit your mother like that!"

"Dad does," he said with a grin.

"That's Dad. Not you."

All kids learn patterns of love and affection from observing their parents. I'm reminded of that every time I see one or another of my sons teasing and displaying affection with his wife just as Ray used to do with me. I'm also reminded of that whenever Michael sneaks up behind me and playfully pops me on my backside. He still does it. I still act irritated with him. And he still always laughs.

I think parents who show affection with each other create an atmosphere of love for the whole family—at least it seemed to work that way in the Jordan home. And even today, with my adult children, our displays of affection for each other are more than a ritual; they're a meaningful reminder of love for all of us.

Like most parents, Ray and I found it easy to be physically affectionate with our small children—to hug, kiss, comfort, snuggle, tickle, and wrestle with them. I think maybe God made these things instinctive because he knew how important such physical interaction is for a child's development.

That's why it bothers me when I hear people say, "You're going to spoil that boy if you don't put him down! Don't be huggin' on him all the time. Babies need to learn to comfort themselves."

That's simply untrue! What little ones need more than anything else in the world is to feel loved. And nothing makes them feel loved any more than physical affection. I don't think we can give our children too much affection any more than I think we can love them too much. It's simply impossible.

Of course, there may come a time when your children think you're giving them too much affection, when they think they've outgrown their need for parental hugs and kisses.

Then you have to learn to adjust, maybe become a little more restrained in your displays of affection. But I don't think you should ever stop showing your love and affection to your kids. When they get too big to cuddle in your lap, you can be alert to natural times for appropriate affectionate contact, perhaps massaging the back of one child's neck as she's studying, giving another's shoulder a loving squeeze as you pass by his place at the table. If you continue to make regular displays of affection a habit, there's a good chance your kids will never outgrow them.

I watched my two daughters grow up without ever tiring of their affectionate father's hugs and kisses. They did reach a point as young women when they got very irritated at his calling them his "little girls," however—or worse yet, his "babies." It especially horrified them when he used such labels in front of their friends. "We're not babies," they'd remind him.

"No matter how old you get, you'll always be my babies," he'd say. They usually had to smile a little at that, but they'd still be irritated.

The boys, too, went through a period of adjustment as young men. While Ray was content to shake their hand and pat them on the back at that stage, their mother expected a little more out of them.

I remember the first time Ronnie came home from the Army. We were all terribly thrilled to have him back. And while he seemed pleased to be home, he acted a little embarrassed by his mother's enthusiastic and affectionate welcome.

So I held him at arm's length and gave him a little talking to. I let him know I realized that he was a man now, and that the Army had been trying to teach him to be strong and tough. But I said, "When you come home, you've got to let the Army go. When I hug you, I expect you to hug me back."

I remember a similar discussion with Larry when he was a teenager. He'd always been a little more shy and reserved than his siblings anyway, so I reminded him that I wanted and needed his affection as a sign of his love. "But you *know* that I love you," he said.

"Then show me. You've had my love and your father's love all your life. We just want you to reach out and give some of that love back."

That wasn't just a selfish request. As much as it meant for me to receive my kids' affection, I knew they also needed to learn to express love naturally and easily. And there's no more basic way, no more important way, to demonstrate our love in a family than through physical affection. Indeed, it's difficult for children to feel loved without a loving touch.

Physical affection can and should be a daily habit. Even if it doesn't come naturally to you—perhaps because you grew up in a family without much—you can learn. Try it; you'll like it!

There's a second way parents can demonstrate their love for their children. I think it's harder than physical affection, but it's every bit as powerful. We prove our love with sacrifice.

Sacrifice isn't a very popular concept these days. It's much more common to read self-help material and other pop psychology that preaches the importance of taking care of ourselves, finding our own unique identity, and discovering personal fulfillment. As nice as all those things may be, by making them seem like the ultimate goal of life, we've validated—even glorified, in some cases—a basic attitude of selfishness.

That seems like such a harsh word, but it's accurate. In talking to parents, in my encounters with children who aren't or don't feel loved, in listening as my own children shared with me the experiences of their friends and the attitudes of some friends' parents, I've become convinced we're experiencing an epidemic of selfishness in our society today. Too many parents have caught the disease. And their children have become the victims, because they aren't ever convinced they're loved.

To paraphrase the old Pillsbury Doughboy jingle, "Nuthin' says lovin' like something *sacrificed*." Good parenting demands sacrifice. *Being there* in the ways we've talked about takes major sacrifice. The time and effort needed to communicate require sacrifice.

We've talked about the commitment called for by parenthood. You could substitute the word *sacrifice* for *commitment* and be saying pretty much the same thing.

Sacrificial love puts others first. Isn't that what parents need to do—at least most of the time? Put children and family first? When we do, it's the most powerful message of love we can possibly give our kids.

Not that our children always or immediately recognize and appreciate all our sacrifices. But those they do recognize, and those they may someday recognize, make for powerful and convincing evidence of our love.

What we're really talking about here is unconditional love. It's not easy. It's the kind of love the Apostle Paul wrote about in 1 Corinthians 13, his famous "love chapter" (verses 4–8, NIV): "Love is patient, love is kind. It does not envy, it does not boast, it is not proud. It is not rude, it is not self-seeking, it is not easily angered, it keeps no record of wrongs. Love does not delight in evil but rejoices with the truth. It always protects, always trusts, always hopes, always perseveres. Love never fails."

That's unconditional love!

If it seems like an impossible standard to live up to, it is. The only hope I see for demonstrating that kind of love for my children is to ask God to help me pursue that goal.

I did that when my kids were young and I still do that, because I want to be sure they know beyond a shadow of a doubt that there's nothing they can ever do to make me stop loving them. I want to believe there's nothing anyone else could ever say or do to make them *think* I don't love them. And I want both my words and my actions to convince them that no one but God could love them any more than I do.

Just a few months ago I found an anonymous poem printed in *Daily Word*, a devotional guide I receive and use every month. I changed some words, rearranged some lines, and sent a copy to each of my children. My revised poem reads like this:

> *You are my beloved child.*
> *Know that I will never forsake you.*
> *I will stand by you even if others have turned their backs*
>   *on you.*
> *I love you unconditionally.*
> *I know what you have gone through and that you did the*
>   *best you knew how to do at the time.*
> *I know your deepest thoughts and desires, and I love you.*
> *I am always ready to listen to you and guide you.*
> *Sometimes you are too distracted to listen, to even know*
>   *that I am there with you,*
> *But I will never leave you or give up on you.*
> *You are my child—a creation of life and love.*
> *There is no one exactly like you.*
> *I will know this is the truth about you even when you*
>   *refuse to know it for yourself.*
> *I love you with a love that knows no bounds.*
> *I will always stand by you.*
>
> *Love, Mom*

That's the kind of love I want to demonstrate to my children. That's the kind of love *all* kids need from their parents.

7

When the Jordan family decided to go to the beach, we always had a choice to make. The closest place (and the one most popular with most folks from Wilmington) was Wrightsville Beach—a long, narrow, dune-covered strip of a barrier island just five to ten minutes' drive from our house. But it was sometimes so crowded we had a hard time finding a spot to spread out our blanket and a harder time yet keeping track of five kids.

If we wanted to take a lazy Sunday afternoon drive, or if we were planning a long, peaceful weekday of sun and sand—especially if we had a carload of cousins on a summertime visit—we'd make the hour-long drive over to Topsail Beach, where the uncrowded sand was just as white and the Atlantic water looked just as blue as at Wrightsville Beach.

More often than not, when we wanted to take the kids for a short swim or a family picnic at a beach, we compromised with the twenty-five-minute drive down to Fort Fisher at the tip of the Cape Fear peninsula. There we could usually find a relatively private expanse of sand to spread out on. If the kids tired of the surf and sunbathing, they could hike around the remains of the historic old Civil War fortification.

The Jordan family never developed much of an interest in swimming. In fact, I've always been a little wary around water—a true landlubber—and I think I passed a lot of that wariness on to my children.

Yet I don't suppose it's possible to grow up where I did in Coastal Carolina, or raise a family as Ray and I did in Wilmington—an old colonial seaport and modern-day naval base—without experiencing something of the flavor, the attraction, and the influence of the sea. That may explain why, whenever I consider all the things a family needs to be, I think in maritime terms. I picture a peaceful harbor, a safe haven for me and for my children; that's what I've always wanted my family to be.

What do I mean by this imagery? What did Ray and I do to try to make our family a safe haven for our five children? How might you accomplish that in your family? Those are the questions I consider in this chapter.

Parents who work at those things we've been talking about in Chapters 3 through 6 have a natural head start in creating a safe haven for their children. When parents make an effort to be there for their kids, their mere presence often serves as a natural breakwater against the most powerful forces and dangers threatening a family. Then, by learning to adapt to and ride out the changing tides, by keeping the communication channels clear and open, and by reaching out and securing their relationships with the unbreakable bonds of unconditional love, they automatically provide much of what's required for a safe haven.

But my image of a family as a safe haven is more than just a byproduct of good, basic parenting strategies. Anyone who has ever spent much time around the harbor of any port city knows those safe havens don't just happen. They're the result of careful attention and intentional action. Channels and river mouths have to be routinely dredged. Moorings, pilings, and piers must be kept in repair. Warning lights, flags, and signs must be persistently monitored and observed. Dockside services must be constantly maintained and improved. And somebody has to be in charge of making sure all that happens. In most seaports that role falls to the harbor master. In a family it has to be the job of the parents.

To be willing to make the effort required to establish and maintain a healthy family atmosphere for their kids, more parents need to understand the benefits that come from providing a safe haven, whether for salty ancient mariners or for tender young children.

Any safe haven serves at least three major roles or purposes. First of all, a safe haven is a place of protection and provision, offering shelter and sanctuary from the dangers of the world. Second, a safe haven is a place of preparation—a secure base from which to boldly venture. And third, a safe haven serves as a familiar refuge you want to return to—a warm place where you can count on always feeling welcome, a relaxing place where you know and are known, a comfortable place where you always belong.

That's a pretty big bill to fill. But I think a family can serve all three purposes. We'll consider them here, one role at a time.

What is it that determines the measure of protection any seaport offers? What is it that makes a haven safe for ships? A deep-water harbor, for starters, and a strong man-made breakwater to hold off damaging waves. Better yet, a high headland or the curve of a bay offering a natural geographic barrier against the force of prevailing winds. In short, any truly safe haven for ships requires some sort of protective structure.

The same is true of safe havens for kids. In order to feel (and be) protected and secure, children need the rock-solid structure families can provide.

What we're really talking about here is discipline — family discipline. Unfortunately, when most parents hear the word *discipline*, they think in terms of punishment and correction. The kind of structure necessary to make families a safe haven for kids requires more than that, however.

In the Jordan household, family structure began with a family schedule.

Many families today — both parents and children — are so busy that there's no normal routine, no daily schedule anyone can count on. Not even a regular bedtime for young children.

A surprising number of parents I talk with today admit that their kids, including toddlers and preschoolers, are often

With my grandson, Cory,
when he was two years old

allowed to stay up until ten, eleven, even midnight. And then those parents wonder why their kids are cranky or disobedient. I want to shake these people awake and say, "Don't you see any connection here?"

My adult children still laughingly complain about the bedtime rules I imposed on them as children. "The sun was still up, we could hear our friends out playing all over the neighborhood, and she had us in bed. Eight o'clock! It was terrible!"

I've already talked about how valuable mealtimes were for communication in our family. They were also an important part of the daily family structure. We would sit down together for supper every evening between five and six. To be sure, there might be an occasional ballgame that interfered. Likewise, outdoor summertime events might dictate on-the-run suppers of hamburgers or hotdogs. And from time to time, Ray would have to stay late working at the plant. But most of the time it was assumed that anyone who expected to eat supper on a given day would be at the supper table with the family. That daily time was so important to the sense of security and well-being in our home that I don't know how a household that doesn't share daily meals can feel like a family.

Indeed, according to a 1995 survey of teenagers listed in *Who's Who in American High Schools*, those kids who join their parents and siblings at the family dinner table are three times as likely to be happy as those who eat alone. Only about half of the students who participated in the survey claimed to regularly share meals with their family. Of those, 79 percent claimed their home life was "happy and close," while that claim was made by only 26 percent of those who ate alone.

Yet another part of the Jordan family's daily schedule took place when the kids arrived home every afternoon. As soon as they'd had an after-school snack, they knew they had to tackle their homework. They couldn't watch TV, play with friends, or do anything else until that homework got done. Schoolwork was simply part of the expected and required daily routine.

Rules, like routine, made up another element of the Jordan family's structure. I realize that rules often become a source of family conflict. Kids may resent having to abide by them, and parents may hate the hassle of enforcing them. I'm not sure which of these is the bigger reason so many families today just don't seem to have any rules.

I remember sitting on the patio behind our house with Ray on warm summer evenings. The two of us would watch with amusement as Larry and Michael meticulously laid out a baseball field in our backyard. The pitcher's mound had to be regulation Little League distance from home; the base-lines had to turn at perfect ninety-degree angles, with the bases exactly sixty feet apart; even the batter's box had to be marked off just like the official one on the field at our local park. Everything had to be just so before the boys and their friends could even start their game.

We laughed at what seemed like childish obsession at the time. But looking back, I see that the boys were learning a very important lesson—a lesson more kids and a lot of parents could benefit from. Without rules to define the game, you can't really play any sport, let alone enjoy it. In fact, whatever sport you're talking about, the players are free to perform at their best only when they know what the expectations are and where the limits stand.

The same thing is true in other areas of life. To enjoy the security and freedom we have in our country, we have to operate by the rules of society. To live life to its fullest and truly enjoy it, we need to abide by those basic rules God lays out for us in the Bible. God isn't out to spoil our good times; our Creator knows full well that life without limits results in chaos and suffering. It's only when we have absolute limits that we can be truly free to experience and enjoy the best that life has to offer.

We tried not to have too many rules in our household, and we tried to relax most rules the older the kids got. But what rules we did have, we expected to be obeyed. Like curfew. Our kids always knew what time they had to be home. They knew that I wasn't going to bed until their feet were through the door. They also knew that if they didn't make it home on time, their parents wouldn't hesitate to go out looking for them.

My daughter Sis discovered just that in what was, to hear her tell it, one of the most embarrassing experiences of her life. When she was maybe sixteen years old, she went to a party at an acquaintance's house. Though I didn't personally know the people hosting the party, I gave Sis permission to go because she told me she would be riding with a friend whose mother was also going to be there. Knowing she was with another adult set my mind at ease.

Until Sis's eleven o'clock curfew came and went, that is. After an hour had passed with no word or sign of her, I got in my car and drove to the party. Sis acted absolutely mortified when I showed up looking for her. She quickly explained that her friend's mother had left the party with her own boyfriend some time earlier and hadn't yet returned. "I didn't have a ride home," she explained.

I assured her I'd give her one. And I suddenly felt a lot less angry with Delois than with the woman I had thought was going to be responsible for my daughter.

I expected all five of my children to abide by the rules Ray and I set. But I admit that we didn't always enforce those rules in the same way with each child. We learned that we had to sometimes adjust the punishment for misbehavior to fit the disposition, personality, and response of the child involved.

We had one son who was always such a responsible boy, so eager to please his parents, that we seldom had to be hard on him. Whenever he felt our displeasure, I could sense his genuine remorse.

Two of our children required a tougher stance than their siblings. With their aggressive personalities, they always seemed to be pushing the limits. We learned to give ground only grudgingly with them. We thought they needed to know that justice would be swift and sure.

The other two required gentler handling, because they seemed so much more sensitive to correction. One was particularly tenderhearted. Just raising my voice with her would so upset her that I seldom had to do more than talk to her when she did something wrong.

However, there were times with all the kids when I felt I had to impose consequences unpleasant enough to discourage certain behavior once and for all. Like Michael's first day of eighth grade at D.C. Virgo Junior High School. At an orientation talk in the school auditorium, the principal announced that students would not be allowed to leave campus during the schoolday. No sooner was the assembly dismissed than Michael and a friend set out for the store across the street to get some candy.

Getting caught earned the boys an automatic three-day suspension from school. A serious sentence. But I was concerned that the idea of being home alone, to do what he wished while his siblings went to school as usual, wouldn't seem enough like punishment to a thirteen-year-old boy. I added a few conditions of my own.

Michael wouldn't spend his suspension at home. If he couldn't go to school, he'd go to work with me instead. I demanded that he bring all his schoolbooks along with him and spend the entire day making up all the work he was missing — and then some. Since I couldn't reasonably expect to have him sit by my desk in the bank for hours, he had to spend the entire day sitting and studying alone in my car. And I parked where I could regularly look out the window to check on him and make sure he was there, working on his studies. I knew that for an active, social kid like Michael such solitary confinement would seem like cruel and unusual punishment. But it worked. He never again got suspended from school.

The teachers I talk to know that the following is true: kids who aren't given any limits at home are more insecure and uncertain, always testing the limits. But those children who have experienced the consequences of misbehavior and have come to accept the structure of rules feel safer and more secure, and they're therefore better able to perform and achieve.

While I usually found it true that the younger my children, the more structure they required in terms of schedule, rules, and punishment, I don't think any of them ever outgrew the need for structure. Larry's first year away at school convinced me of that. He had such a difficult adjustment that he never really settled into college life that freshman year.

Larry had always been such a homebody. Unlike his younger brother, Michael, he seldom wanted even to spend the night at a friend's house. So I concluded after his rough first year that he would enjoy college a lot more if he were in a homelike setting. Before his sophomore year, we found a place off campus—a couple willing to take in a student who would have his own room and share living and kitchen space with their family. Larry lived with those folks the rest of his time at school. He was comfortable and secure there because the place felt less like a dorm and more like a safe haven, a home—because that's exactly what it was.

But a good safe haven, whether for boats or for children, offers more than protection and security. It also serves that second function as a place of preparation and provision—a secure base from which to boldly venture.

So many children are not being provided for today. We see their stories all too often in the news—horrible, heart-wrenching stories of suffering children. My work with the foundation often brings me face-to-face with some of them. The clinging little girl at the F.A.O. Schwarz Christmas party who'd been living on the winter sidewalks of Chicago. The rambunctious little boy enjoying free run of his hospital ward after living much of his life locked in a dark closet.

There's such an epidemic of child abuse and neglect in our society that to some degree we've all become desensitized to it. What's even worse, I fear it's caused many well-meaning and responsible parents to lower their standards. When so many other parents fail to provide for the most basic of needs, it's easy to feel as if we must be doing a pretty good job if we're offering food, clothing, and shelter. We content ourselves as parents with meeting our children's basic physical needs and forget that that's only part of the provision they require.

What are the most important lessons children need to learn to cope with modern life? Who's going to teach them if parents don't? Where better to learn those lessons than at home?

More parents need to catch this vision of the family as a safe haven in which to deliberately prepare and equip children today for the challenges that lie out there in the open water of tomorrow. We should see the family as a training camp where we review the fundamentals and fine-tune the strategies we plan to use later. A laboratory in which to discover and examine life's most important truths. A safe testing ground where children can experience life and relationships in a controlled setting.

In Chapters 9 and 10 I take a look at a few of the important provisions I wanted all my children to have—gifts I wished to bestow in order to equip them for a successful, productive and happy journey through life. We'll talk some in Chapter 10 about what the Jordans did to try to provide those critical resources.

But none of that provisioning, none of the preparation carried out in the safe haven of our families, will do any good unless we encourage and enable our children to sail from our safe harbor and venture out into the world. They need encouragement, reinforcement, and affirmation of worthy goals. Offering this affirmation of their dreams is one of the most important roles we as parents can fulfill.

All of my children have pursued their own dreams. Some of those dreams, like Ronnie's plan for a military career, have been achieved. Others, like Ros's goal of success in the music and songwriting business, are yet to be realized. But in every case, Ray and I saw ourselves as providers of encouragement, letting our children know that we believed in them and their abilities and urging them to give their best in pursuit of those dreams no matter the odds.

I'll never forget the summer day Michael walked into the kitchen excited about having just watched television coverage of the basketball competition for the 1972 Olympic Games in Munich. "Someday I'm going to play basketball in the Olympics!" he announced.

"Oh, really?" I asked with a smile.

"I'm going to win a gold medal!" he declared.

I don't remember exactly what I said in response. I *do* know, though, that it was positive in tone. Something like, "I'm sure you will," or "Wouldn't that be great?" Although I considered Michael's declaration nothing more than a small boy's big talk, I didn't want to say anything to belittle him or discourage the dream. It's a good thing too. For while I soon put the incident out of my mind, Michael never forgot his vow to become an Olympian.

After the horn sounded the end of the gold medal game at the 1984 Summer Games in Los Angeles, Michael raced up into the cheering crowd, lifted me off my feet, and swung me around and around in the crowded aisle in joyous celebration as I screamed and we both laughed. When he put me down, he reminded me of what I'd long forgotten: what he'd said in the kitchen that day in 1972. Realizing how that memory must have helped motivate Michael for all those years, I was unspeakably thankful I hadn't said anything to make him think I didn't believe in him or his dream. A negative response on my part could have snuffed out that tiny, first flickering flame of his ambition almost before it got burning.

Instead, he felt that his parents were such a part of his dream that he wanted us to share the excitement of his gold medal achievement. Realizing that made our little celebration in the stands one of the happiest, most rewarding moments I've ever known as a parent. And it convinced me once and for all that nurturing dreams has to be a crucial part of the preparation families and parents provide for their children.

A safe haven isn't just a place of protection and a place of preparation. It must also be a familiar place you can always return to—a place where you know you'll be welcome, where you're known, where you simply belong.

As a mother, I don't know that there was anything that ever warmed my heart more than the look of happiness and peace I saw on my children's faces when they walked in the door after another long day away at school. They always seemed so glad to return to the familiar surroundings of home.

But if you want children to view your home as a safe haven, you have to work to foster such feelings. When my kids were small, I felt it important to do that by being there to welcome them with a warm hug and a snack when they got home.

Ray and I did what we could to make our home a gathering place. We wanted everyone to feel welcome. So I was always happy to hear one of my kids say to a friend, "Why don't you come over to our house for supper? My mother can always fix enough for one more."

Ray built the basketball court in our backyard with much the same attitude. He wanted a place the kids would want to bring their friends to. It worked: we provided a welcome place for our children and attracted a lot of other kids from the neighborhood as well.

Now that my children are adults and have established their own homes, I still want my house to be a welcome place for them and their families. Seeing the look of peaceful pleasure on their faces when they walk through my door remains one of the greatest joys of my life.

Food still plays a major part in the equation as well. No sooner do my children get in my house than they ask, "What did you cook, Mother?" Macaroni and cheese and my sweet potato casserole always seem to be popular choices.

I realize that not every family enjoys such experiences. I think it's terribly sad when I hear people complain about having to get together with relatives. For me and for my children, the highlights of every year are those times when we can get together as a family to share a simple meal and enjoy the pleasure of each other's company.

Our family is still a safe haven where we can share joys and burdens and decisions. For Michael especially, with his celebrity and constant media attention, family offers a place like no other—a peaceful, welcome refuge away from the eyes of the world.

At the same time Michael was wrestling with his decision to retire from basketball back in 1993, Ronnie was trying to decide whether or not to re-up for another tour of duty with the Army. I had two thirty-something sons contemplating retirement at the same time. I'd never felt so old. But what encouraged me was seeing how much each of them sought the input of the other for his decision. Ronnie would say to Michael, "I think you need to consider this." And Michael would tell his older brother, "Are you sure you've considered that?" It heartened me to realize that they saw family as an important place to return to for wisdom and advice.

In the wake of Ray's death, whenever we've gotten together as a family these last couple years, we've shared much pain and even more memories. In the process we've found mutual strength and a large measure of healing.

And we've discovered anew how important it is for all of us to have the safe haven of family to turn and return to once again.

I've lost count of the number of basketball games I've watched Michael play. I've been to hundreds in person and watched hundreds more on television—over a thousand in all, I suppose. And yet I'm still just as amazed as everyone else by the sometimes unfathomable things he can accomplish on a basketball court.

Maybe more so, because he's my son. He's just Michael.

When people praise him as "the greatest who ever played the game of basketball," I remember the heartbroken high school sophomore who came home to tell me he'd been cut from the varsity team. When Michael somehow soars, twists, and hangs in the air on another one of his gravity-defying slam dunks to ignite a coliseum full of fans and tongue-tied commentators trying to describe what they've just seen, I remember those months of frustration in our backyard court when his brother Larry could dunk a ball and Michael still couldn't. While I know he's a genuine superstar today, known and admired by untold millions of people around the world, I remember holding him in my arms as a newborn baby and trying to imagine what his future would hold.

In the years since then, I've watched him achieve so many impressive goals. A national championship in college, two Olympic gold medals, three straight NBA championships, annual All-Star appearances, seven straight NBA scoring titles, multiple most-valuable-player awards, and so much more that I can only shake my head in amazement and pride as I realize how long and hard he's worked for it all.

But I've been even more proud when Michael has admitted, in response to questions by countless interviewers about one or all of his accomplishments, "I couldn't have done it alone," and then has given credit to others—whether family, friends, or teammates. I felt especially good when I read what he said in his 1994 book *I Can't Accept Not Trying*: "Talent wins games, but teamwork and intelligence win championships."

I hope he learned that at home. I know I certainly did.

After almost four decades as a mother, I'm convinced that there's no way to win at the parenting game without teamwork. And the broader your support network, the better. The job of parenting is too complicated, too demanding, and too important for anyone to try to do it all alone. I never could have done it by myself.

Raising my five kids was truly a big-team effort. But the support network I developed over the years began and ended at

Larry, Roslyn, Michael, Ronnie, and me at the Michael Jordan Foundation
Gala Event raising money for charities, 1993

home, with Ray. I married a man who believed in family and always wanted to be a partner in raising our children. For more than thirty-five years we were a parenting team.

I realize I was fortunate in this regard. I also know that in America today there are more single parents raising children than at any other time in history. And that troubles me, because so many of the neediest children the Michael Jordan Foundation works with in schools and communities around the country come from single-parent homes.

I'm not meaning to imply that all the problems I see with kids today are the result of single-parent families. And I certainly don't want to imply that single-parent families are destined to produce problem children. A lot of single parents do an admirable job of putting their family first. Many put me to shame in doing all the important things I've been talking about in these last few chapters—being there for their children, adapting to their kids' changing needs, communicating their unconditional love, and creating a safe haven for learning and growth.

But as much as I want to applaud and encourage caring single parents, I remain convinced that when the Lord determined it would take two human beings to conceive a child, he fully expected it would take both of them to raise that child. While no marriage is perfect (mine certainly wasn't), God's biblical idea of marriage remains the best pattern ever devised for creating and raising healthy and happy children.

It's simple arithmetic: two is always more than one. One big job divided into two smaller parts is easier to get done. A load pulled by two people is lighter for both than that same load pulled by either alone. Whatever or however many strengths two people have, they add up to more than the strength of either individual. So a marriage partnership can and should be a big plus when it comes to parenting.

It was for Ray and me.

Even our differences often added up to an advantage. When a parenting challenge came up, we automatically had two viewpoints on how we might respond. Sometimes we'd end up going my way, sometimes his. But as often as not, we'd talk until we found a middle road that incorporated the best ideas of both.

I was an encourager, while Ray was more of a pusher. I'd tell the kids what a great job they were doing and how proud I was of them. Ray, on the other hand, always had a suggestion about how they might improve their performance next time. As a result of our combined approaches, all five of our kids grew up feeling both affirmed in their abilities and challenged to do their best.

I was in some ways a stereotypical mother—tending toward protectiveness and caution, worrying about the safety and well-being of my children. Ray was more adventurous, a little more willing to allow for experience and experiment; his attitude was regularly reflected in words such as, "They'll be fine. Everything will be all right." Here again I think our combined tendencies added up to an advantage: we provided a safe and secure home, yet we allowed our kids a healthy variety of experiences growing up.

For example, I think we both felt pretty good about the ponies we bought for our kids when Larry, Michael, and

Roslyn were just starting school. We figured feeding, grooming, and caring for the animals would teach the children something about responsibility, while learning to ride would give them a sense of fun and adventure.

How much and what kind of adventure they had I didn't find out until very recently, at a family get-together where my adult children were reminiscing about those ponies. It seems Larry and Michael, as young as they were, never felt completely satisfied by the speed at which those short-legged ponies galloped. Not only did they wish those little animals would run faster, but they also wanted their reluctant ponies to jump obstacles—logs and ditches, for example—in the woods where the kids rode. They tried everything they'd ever seen television cowboys do to get extra performance out of their mounts, but to no avail. Until one day one of them—I don't know that they ever admitted which one—grabbed hold of a pony's tail and pulled. The animal's sudden burst of movement gave them an idea, which they hastened to put into practice. After one of them mounted up, the other would get a firm grip on the pony's tail and give a sharp yank. That poor angry pony would run faster and jump higher than he'd ever gone in his life.

If I'd known what lengths Michael and Larry went to in order to make their ponies jump, I'd have been even more reluctant to get them that dirt bike they wanted when they were twelve and thirteen. Ray pointed out that some of the other kids in the neighborhood already had motorbikes and that the twelve acres of woods we owned behind our house would be a nice, safe place to ride. "They'll be okay," he assured me.

Looking back now, I wonder if Ray knew about the ponies. Or maybe he just knew boys. In any event, I remember his being very clear and stern in his warning to the boys that their bike wasn't to be used for jumping. "Not only might you tear up the bike; you could get seriously hurt," he told them.

The kids did enjoy that bike. And I think they made a conscientious effort to be careful and responsible — at least for a while.

I don't remember how long we had the dirt bike. Long enough that I quit worrying about it very much, yet not so long that I wouldn't keep an ear out for the distant whine of the engine winding around back in the woods while I worked in the kitchen. One summer evening when I asked Ray to call the boys in for supper, I commented, "I haven't heard their bike for some time now."

"Maybe they ran out of gas," Ray replied as he headed out to the backyard and bellowed into the woods, "Suppertime, boys!"

Still no sound of the bike starting. "Where are they?" I asked when Ray came back inside.

"I heard them call from way in the back corner of the property," he said, "so they're coming."

We decided the rest of us would sit down and start eating while the food was hot. Sure enough, a few minutes later the back door opened and the boys slipped hurriedly through the kitchen and up the stairs. One called over his shoulder, "Sorry we're late. We had to push the bike back"; from the other we heard, "We've got to go get washed up."

I thought it a little odd that they had disappeared upstairs so quickly. After all, they could have washed their hands at the kitchen sink. Several more minutes passed before they rather quietly took their places at the table.

I knew something was wrong. *But what?* Then I realized Larry seemed to be holding one of his arms awkwardly in his lap, below table level and out of sight. It wasn't until he reached for seconds that I caught sight of the big skinned patch on his arm.

"What happened to you?" I asked in alarm as I bent to examine his arm. Larry looked at Michael before he responded, and I suddenly realized Michael was holding one of his arms at an odd angle as well. Both boys had cuts, bruises, and huge raw patches of forearm where the skin had been scraped off.

"We had a little accident with the bike," one of them admitted. "That's why we had to push it back to the house," the other one volunteered.

"How did it happen?" Ray wanted to know. "You were jumping the bike, weren't you? Where?"

To their credit, they admitted the truth. They'd built a dirt ramp and had tried to soar Evel Knievel-style over a small canal running across the back of our property. With both of them on the bike, they failed to clear the ditch.

"You know you could have broken your necks?" I said.

"After I warned you boys not to jump that bike?" Ray queried ominously.

"Yes, sir. We know," they replied quietly.

We grounded this early, motorized version of the Air Jordan boys. They couldn't ride in the woods for some time after that. And soon after we rescinded the punishment and they got the bike up and running again, they decided to sell the thing. I had no regrets about that.

Remembering that incident and imagining what could have happened, I'm reminded that even with two parents working as a team, you can't always protect your children from harm. That's all the more reason for parents to develop a broad support network.

In addition to Ray, I found our extended family an invaluable resource in my parenting experience. My own mother died rather suddenly when Ronald and Sis were still tiny, so I never got to call on her expertise as much as I'd have liked. But Ray's mother, Rosabell Jordan—whom I always called Ms. Bell—was a constant source of parenting wisdom and advice. Early in our marriage, when I felt most insecure as a new mother, we lived right across the road from her. When Ronnie developed a rash or Sis got fussy and wouldn't eat, I'd call Ms. Bell and she'd walk over to see what she thought might be wrong.

Even after we moved thirty-eight miles away to Wilmington, we maintained close and regular contact with Ray's family. Every Sunday we drove back to Wallace for church, then ate Sunday dinner and spent a long, leisurely afternoon visiting with Ms. Bell and whatever other relatives happened to be there that day. When the kids were little, Ms. Bell answered all my questions about everything from vaccinations to the differences in potty training between girls and boys. Whether it was Michael's kindergarten year, when I didn't know who else to share my worries about his classroom behavior with (Michael was driving his teacher to distraction: he constantly got up and moved around the room when his teacher wanted him to sit quietly in his seat), or later, when I had teenagers and was willing to talk to anyone who might have helpful advice, Ms. Bell was there. And she was always eager to listen and willing to share from her lifetime treasure of experience. I can't count the number of times she eased my mind by saying, "Ray used to do the very same thing," or "I had a friend whose daughter had a similar problem." Often it was her calm, matter-of-fact, this-isn't-so-bad-and-everything-will-be-fine attitude that helped as much as her advice.

Ms. Bell always enjoyed having her grandchildren come and stay with her overnight, or for several days at a time during the summer. In what became an annual family tradition, we'd eat Thanksgiving dinner at her house and then Ray and I would leave all the kids in Wallace with her for the remainder of the holiday weekend. We'd drive to Atlanta or New York to have a few days by ourselves and get a jump on our Christmas shopping.

While Ray's mom played an important role in our lives, she wasn't the only relative to do so. My father, my older brothers and sisters, and Ray's sisters were not just valued members of our extended family; I considered them all part of my parenting support network.

When I was a little girl growing up in rural North Carolina, everyone in our little community always seemed to know everyone else's business. And what's more, they took an interest in and a certain amount of responsibility for each other's children. If I was playing at a friend's house and we got into some trouble that her parents thought earned her a switchin', I'd get a switchin' too. And if any one of the neighbor ladies on our block caught me doing something she knew my parents wouldn't approve of, I knew I was in trouble. She might just chastise me herself, or she might report to my folks, who would punish me.

Things had changed quite a bit by the time I was raising my children. I don't think many parents I knew would have felt free to punish someone else's children. But in the stable, middle-class neighborhoods where we raised our family, there were always a number of friends and neighbors who knew one another well enough to feel responsible and help keep an eye out for each other's children. I appreciated those people who took the time and made the effort to speak to my children or let me know when one of mine was going somewhere or doing something I'd be concerned about. Since I couldn't be everywhere in the neighborhood at once, I considered these members of the community a valued part of my support network as well.

For me as a parent, another very valuable source of support was Dr. William Sutton. Like many in my generation, I got my share of child-rearing advice from books by the likes of Dr. Spock. But when I couldn't get reassuring answers from books or from more experienced family members, I turned to my own personal pediatrics expert: Dr. Sutton, our family doctor.

I'll never forget the time I put a sleeping baby Michael down on the middle of our big bed. He was quick even then, because I was out of the room only a few moments before I heard a sudden scream. When I ran back into the room and couldn't see Michael anywhere, I panicked. Then I heard him scream again. He'd rolled off the far side of the mattress and had wedged himself between the bed and the wall. When I reached down and pulled him out, his face was covered with blood.

I didn't even bother getting dressed. I ran out the door carrying Michael in my arms and drove straight to Dr. Sutton's office, where I made quite an entrance in my robe and slippers, cradling a bloody infant and screaming at the nurse, "You've got to help me! Something is wrong with my baby!"

Dr. Sutton came rushing out to check on the commotion. "What happened?" he asked as he quickly began examining Michael. By the time I'd finished explaining, he had visibly relaxed and looked up with a reassuring smile. "He's going to be fine," he told me. "I know it looks terrible, but he's got just a bloody nose."

When Ronnie returned from a tour of duty in Korea and I worried about his health, I said, "Go see Dr. Sutton to make sure you're okay."

From my children's births to their adulthood, Dr. Sutton was our family doctor and more. Over the years he became a personal friend, a confidant, and a true supporter of our family and of me as a parent.

I know that in this day of huge HMOs and twenty-four-hour-a-day walk-in clinics, a lot of people seldom see the same doctor more than once or twice. Very few people have a traditional family doctor anymore—especially one who cares for a family for twenty years or more.

I also know that in our modern, mobile society there are millions of families who never know and are never known by their neighbors. And there are millions more who have little or no regular contact with any extended family.

So many parents today—perhaps the majority—don't have the full benefit of the medical, community, and extended-family support I could always count on as a parent. When you consider that, and then factor in the number of single parents who can't count on their spouse's partnership, it makes the remaining elements of my parenting support network even more important.

One of the best sources of parental support I found in raising my kids was something every parent can and should utilize: the public education system. Every one of my children's teachers, every principal and every counselor of every school they ever attended, knew who I was. I introduced myself at the very first opportunity and enlisted them on my parenting team by letting them know I wanted them to consider me part of their educational team. I figured if they saw that I cared enough about what they were doing to help them achieve their goals, then I could count on their cooperation and input toward my goals as a parent.

I not only volunteered to do whatever I could to help them out in the classroom, I always let them know my own concerns and goals for my children. I didn't just sign my kids' report cards; I sent them back annotated with comments and reactions: "I'm encouraged that Larry is doing so well in math, but I think he ought to be doing better in English. Please let me know what he needs to be working on and what I might do to help him bring up his grades."

I currently serve as a board member of North Carolina Cities in Schools, a group that works to prevent dropouts. I know that most public school personnel are overworked and underpaid. They're responsible for so many students with so many needs that even the best and most caring of them can't do everything that could and should be done for each child. The same was true when my kids were growing up.

But my experience has taught me (and the educators our foundation works with confirm that this is still true) that the surest way to make certain your child's educational needs will be met, that he won't slip through the cracks in the system, that teachers and administrators will see that she gets that extra help required to succeed in school, is for you to get involved. Not just by being there (though that's important) but by letting educators know you're willing to be part of their educational team—volunteering to help at the school office or in a classroom an hour a week, going as an extra adult chaperone on a daughter's field trip, or tutoring your son a few extra hours in his weakest subject.

Educators notice parents who make the effort to be part of their support team. Naturally they then notice and pay particular attention to the needs of those parents' children. And in the process, they become a concerned and valuable part of the parenting support network.

A great many teachers went the extra mile for me and my children over the years. Michael had an instructor at Laney High who felt he wasn't being challenged enough in math. She went out of her way to arrange for him to enroll in an afternoon trigonometry course on the campus of nearby UNC-Wilmington during his final semester of high school.

When I didn't know how to advise my teenagers on something, or when we had differing opinions about something important, there was usually some teacher that they respected and I trusted to whom we could turn. And I'd feel comfortable asking, "Have you talked to Mrs. Newsome about this?" or "Maybe you should stop by the counseling office and see if Ms. Moore has any thoughts on that."

I know I didn't hesitate to talk to everyone I could at Laney High when Roslyn decided she wanted to head off to college after her junior year. I discussed the issue with the principal, the school's guidance counselors, and a number of teachers. They all had pretty much the same reaction. While they empathized with my concern about sending a sixteen-year-old girl off to college, they all told me she was academically ready. They also felt she was emotionally mature enough to handle college life. The reassurance I received from the educators at Laney High gave me the confidence and sense of peace I needed to make it through that difficult transition.

As much involvement and input as we wanted to have in our kids' lives, Ray and I knew we couldn't and shouldn't be their only adult role models. Scout leaders were among the people who naturally served that function for our kids. Other responsible adults who were involved in leading and providing kids' activities in the community likewise became a part of our parenting support network.

The kids' coaches always played a significant role in their lives and in the life of our family, from the kids' days playing Little League baseball at the local Optimist Club fields right on through college athletics.

Perhaps the biggest reason Ray and I felt good about Michael's decision to accept a basketball scholarship at North Carolina was that we had so much confidence in Coach Dean Smith and his staff. They didn't just coach basketball; they shared our concern as parents for the overall well-being and development—emotional, social, and scholastic—of their players.

And that sensitivity to the feelings and concerns of families extended beyond the players themselves. The UNC coaching staff not only gave us regular progress reports on Michael; they checked on Roslyn and kept me updated on her adjustment to college as well. There were actually a few times when I felt better informed about what my two youngest children were doing when they were off in Chapel Hill than when they were living at home with me in Wilmington. Coach Guthridge, one of Dean Smith's assistants, and Dean himself, who became a second father figure for Michael, played a huge part in our family support system while our kids were in college.

I was always so involved with the daily demands of my own growing family that I never seemed to find time to develop and pursue a lot of best-friend, let's-get-together-and-do-something relationships with other women. Most of the adult friendships I found over the years were the more casual variety that developed around my family's activities. Someone I carpooled with, the mother on the next block whose kids came over to play, and the parents of my kids' teammates— people we'd sit and talk with in the stands and maybe travel with to games in other parts of the state or across the country. Ray and I developed some wonderful friendships with the other parents who accompanied the North Carolina team on an exhibition tour of Greece one summer.

All my children's lives, I've tried to make a special point of not only getting to meet the kids' friends and teammates but getting to know the parents and families of their friends as well. Simply because we shared mutual interests, many of those parents became longtime friends whom I also viewed as important sources of encouragement and support for me as a parent.

Parents need other parents as friends.

Another very important place I found support as a parent was at church. Our pastors not only offered me spiritual guidance but often shared their own personal parenting experience and wisdom whenever I went to them for advice—which seemed quite often, especially during those troublesome teenage years.

I also discovered a real sense of support and encouragement among many of the other believers with whom I fellowshiped regularly at church. While that was in part because many of them were also parents, I think there's more to it than shared life experiences.

The church's primary reason for existence is to meet the needs of others, to minister to those who are hurting or lost.

I've been in enough churches to realize that some congregations do a lot better at fulfilling their God-given mission than others. And certainly no church is perfect.

But the millions of parents who are letting that reason, or any other reason, keep them from being involved in a local church are missing out on what I think is one of the most valuable resources available for parenting today. Not only can we as parents always benefit from spiritual guidance, but the caring, compassionate people we meet and worship with can become a natural part of our parenting support network.

Most parents need all the help they can get. I did. The preceding passages describe just some of the people and places where I found it.

I talk to enough parents and families these days to understand that things are very different from when I was raising my children. While I know our world is changing fast, I still believe most parents can find invaluable help in many of the same places I did.

First you have to realize that parenting isn't something anyone can manage alone. Then you can begin to build the supportive team network every successful parent needs.

CHAPTER 9

Several times recently I've had people ask me, "What in the world do you give Michael for his birthday or for Christmas? What kind of gift can you give someone who has so much and can afford to buy himself almost anything he wants?"

This past year I gave him a watch that had belonged to his father. It made me feel wonderful when Michael said, "Thank you, Mother. You couldn't have given me anything that would have meant more."

I've now given each of my children something I've taken from a chest of Ray's things, because I know how special it is for them to have something of their father's.

In the past, when I've wanted to find unique and meaningful gifts for my children, I've gone to my attic and pulled out a memento of their childhood—a school art project, a certificate of achievement, a memorable letter written from camp or college, or a sweet note they had included in a

Mother's Day card. I've found a frame or some other appropriate way to display the memento and have presented the gift with a personal note from me. The kids seem to appreciate these little surprises, and I enjoy both the sharing of the memories and the knowledge that I've given them something no one else in the world could give them.

As parents, we give our children a lot of things over the years—at Christmas, on birthdays, and on countless other occasions. We spend much time, energy, thought, and money in our attempts to make these gifts special.

In this chapter and the next, I suggest some gift ideas parents might consider in an attempt to make their *children* special. Unlike the toys and games we assemble after midnight every Christmas Eve, or the birthday presents we hide in the closet weeks ahead of time, these are gifts our children can take with them when they leave home and can benefit from all their lives.

Most of these may seem like a natural outgrowth of the parenting strategies we've covered in Chapters 3 through 8, and indeed they are. But what we've been talking about so far is parenting tools—goals and guidelines we can set for ourselves as we carry out our roles as mothers and fathers.

What we're talking about in this chapter and the next is the results we're aiming for, the aspirations we have for our children, the character traits we hope they'll develop, and the goals we hope they'll reach.

Every parent has his or her list of these important, lasting gifts we want our children to acquire. I'll share just a few of mine—and I'll highlight each one with a hodgepodge of related stories, opinions, observations, comments, and quotes drawn from Jordan family experience.

CONCERN FOR OTHERS

I think it's easier for a child in a big family to learn consideration for others than it is for a child with no (or few) siblings. When you're one of five, the natural experience of give-and-take teaches you that you can't be the center of the universe—at least not for long.

Children with no siblings have to learn this hard lesson out in the world, and that can be rough.

What better place than the family to practice and develop a concern for others? I remember Ronnie coming home from school one day and complaining that he hadn't been able to buy something he'd taken extra money for—maybe ice cream at lunch—because Sis had had to buy pencils at the school store and needed his change to make her purchase.

"She had a right to expect your help," I told him. "We're a family. We share. Not just here at home, but when we go out in the world. We know we can depend on each other. If we couldn't depend on each other, we couldn't depend on anyone. You're your brothers' and your sisters' keeper."

There are plenty of opportunities to develop this theme in most families.

But concern for others needs to extend beyond those closest to us.

Driving home from church one night up in Wallace, we got behind an old, slow-moving truck that was weaving all over the road. Ray wanted to pass, but the prospect looked too risky.

"Watch out," I warned. "That driver must be drunk!"

"I think you may be right," Ray agreed. "He shouldn't even be on the road."

With that, Ray sped up and tried to get around the truck. When it swerved, Ray braked suddenly enough to scare the kids and me. Slowly Ray again eased up close to the back of the truck and then tried to accelerate around. This time we managed to pull alongside, and Ray motioned the driver over to the shoulder as we sped past and then gradually slowed down. Ray watched in the rearview mirror. When the driver of the truck had coasted to the edge of the road and stopped, Ray pulled over and backed our car almost to the truck's front bumper. Then he climbed out of the car and walked back to the driver's window.

With an air of friendly concern, he said to the elderly black gentleman driving the truck, "I saw you weaving all over the road back there and wondered if maybe something was wrong."

I couldn't hear much of what the fellow said, but he was clearly in no condition to drive. Ray kept talking to him until he had convinced the old man to leave his truck parked beside the road for the night and let us give him a ride home.

The moment the man climbed in the backseat with the kids, I knew what the problem was, and so did they. Every time I looked back I could see the kids (Ronnie was about fourteen at the time, so the youngest three were ten and under) making faces at me and covering their noses to ward off the nearly overpowering smell of alcohol.

We drove only a few miles out of our way to take the old guy home. But even as we watched him stagger up the steps to his front door, the kids began to complain. "That man smelled awful! Did you have to put him in the backseat with us? Why did you make him come with us, Daddy?"

Ray said, "We may have just saved that man's life. Perhaps we also saved the life of a family in a car he would have run into down the road. I just couldn't let him cause an accident."

They understood that. "But did you have to put him back here with us?"

I laughed. "Better that than up here with me."

I've remembered that incident many times over the years and thought about what their father's action said to our five kids about concern for others.

Ray was always doing things like that—stopping alongside the road or chasing across town to help someone who had broken down.

Whatever you call it—concern for others, compassion, generosity—I think most children have to learn it from their parents' example. When I gave a neighbor without a car a ride to the grocery store, when I took a meal to someone who'd been sick, I hope my deeds were an example to my children.

I like to think Michael's enthusiastic support—both financial and otherwise—of so many worthy causes, and all my children's willing participation in the work of our foundation, is due at least in part to the concern for others they witnessed in their parents.

STRONG SELF-IDENTITY

I always told my kids, "Don't be a follower; be a leader." I was also fond of saying, "If you know who you are, you can always keep your balance in this world."

I also told my children, "Don't let other people limit you with their expectations of you. Don't allow others to steal your choices by making decisions for you. Don't let other people steal your brains by doing your thinking for you."

Another favorite bit of wisdom: "If you're comfortable with yourself, you can be comfortable in any situation or setting."

Despite living in the small-town South, our family experienced surprisingly little racial prejudice. Most of the time, if it was there, we paid it very little attention.

I do remember Michael coming home from school one day when he was quite young and telling me that a girl on the bus had called him an ugly racial name. He'd gotten angry, snatched her glasses off, and thrown them out the bus window.

"You know," I told him, "I don't think that girl even knew what she was saying. I doubt she even knows what that word means. Do *you* know what it really means? It's a word used for someone who's ignorant. Is that what you are?"

He shook his head.

"Then she wasn't talking about you at all. *She* was the one being ignorant. You shouldn't let anything she said get you upset or determine how you react." We went back and found the girl's glasses, and I went with Michael the next morning when he returned them.

Another time Michael went over to a white friend's house to go swimming in a backyard pool. When he came home, I could tell something was eating at him, so I asked what was wrong. He told me that when he and his buddy had gotten in the pool, everyone else had immediately gotten out. "Was that because I'm black?" he asked.

"I don't know," I told him honestly, "and you won't *ever* know for sure. But I do know that since you were invited to your friend's house, you had every right anyone else had to be swimming. If your color was the reason the other people got out of the pool, it was their problem, not yours. You're every bit as good as they are, and you can't let their attitude affect you."

"No one is better than you." I told my kids that a lot.

This past summer, just prior to the second anniversary of Ray's death, I found a poem titled "Your Name." Written by Edgar A. Guest, it contained a sentiment I thought appropriate for James Ronald, the son I named after his daddy. I adapted it and sent it to him, addressed to "Ronnie":

> You got it from us, your parents. 'Twas the best we had to
> give,
> And right gladly we bestowed it—it is yours all while you
> live.
> You may lose some things we gave you and some others
> you may claim,
> But remember, when you're tempted, to be careful of your
> name.
> It was fair the day you got it and a worthy name to wear.
> When I vowed to take it from your father, there was no dis-
> honor there;
> Through the years we proudly wore it, to his father we were
> true,
> And that name was clean and spotless when we passed it
> on to you.
> Oh, there's much that we have given that we valued not
> at all.
> We watched you break your playthings in the days when
> you were small,
> You've lost some things we gave you, and we loved you just
> the same.

*But you'll never hurt me as a parent if you're careful of our
  name.*
It is yours to wear forever, yours to wear all while you live,
*Yours, perhaps, some distant morning to another child to
  give,*
*And you'll smile as do your parents smile, above the baby
  there,*
*If a clean name and a good name you are giving him to
  wear.*

I signed it simply "Love always, Mom."

PERSEVERANCE

I always told my kids, "In order to achieve anything worthwhile, you've got to work hard and earn it. If someone gives
you something for nothing, it's not really yours.

"To grow, you have to work hard, discipline yourself, and
set goals."

Anytime one of my children said, "I can't do that," I
would ask, "How do you know? Have you tried? Don't ever
tell me you can't do something unless you've tried! You aren't
a failure just because you fail at something you attempt to do.
You're a failure only when you fail to try. There should be no
shame in falling short of your goal, as long as you know you've
done your very best.

"Every successful person has failed at some time in his or
her life. If you haven't failed, you may not be trying hard

enough; you may not be setting your goals high enough. Most of us learn by failing. Failures actually strengthen us."

DREAMS AND GOALS

It's important for parents to encourage their children to dream. But if you want to help your kids achieve their dreams, you've got to teach them to set goals.

From the time our children were small, Ray and I talked to them about goals—small goals, short-term goals, and long-term goals. Our goal-setting habit started with sports: "What's your goal in the game tonight?"

"I'm going to get at least two hits," or "I'm going to score fourteen points!"

But goal setting certainly wasn't limited to sports. We encouraged it in all areas of life. "I'm going to read this stack of library books in the next two weeks," or "I'm going to make the honor roll this next semester."

"And how do you intend to do that?" we would ask. (There needs to be a plan for pursuing and achieving each goal.)

"Well, I'm going to spend extra time each day doing extra math assignments, since algebra is the one class that kept me off the honor roll last time."

Most kids need help balancing short-term and long-term goals. As important as it is to look and think ahead, it's just as important to enjoy and learn from what you're doing today.

I remember Michael coming home one weekend during his freshman year of college and telling us that someone had mentioned the possibility of his playing in the NBA someday. I cautioned him, "Don't worry about the NBA yet. It's time now to concentrate on getting an education. You're still adjusting to college life. Let's deal with that and not look too far ahead."

Education needs to be part of every dream, and it was certainly one of our most important goals for our children. We made it such a priority that not one of my children ever considered dropping out. That was simply never an option. My kids understood that if they wanted to be strong people — the kind of people who could make a difference in the world — they had to have a good education.

I told my kids, "No matter where you go or what happens to you in life, no one can ever take an education away from you."

INTEGRITY

When they were still living at home, I often reminded my kids, "Your word is your bond." If they made an agreement, whether it was to give a sibling a dime in exchange for a candy bar or to give a friend their bike in exchange for cold hard cash, they needed to keep their bargain — even if the candy bar turned out to be stale or the bike was sorely missed the next day. In other words, even if they decided that a prior agreement wasn't in their best interest, they needed to realize that honesty was *always* in their best interest. There's never enough money to buy integrity.

A number of sportswriters made a big deal out of the fact that Michael never went back to the Bulls' management and asked them to rewrite his long-term contract for more money. Even though he was considered the best player in the game and a long list of other players around the NBA were getting paid millions more than he was, I knew he'd never do such a thing. His word was his bond.

He shows the same kind of commitment to his word when it comes to the products he endorses. When he was a spokesman for Coca-Cola, for example, he wouldn't drink any other soft drink. What's more, he wouldn't let the rest of the family drink anything else either!

During his endorsement of Coke, an orange juice company approached me about doing a television commercial. When I mentioned the possibility to Michael, he said, "You can't do that! Coca-Cola owns Minute Maid. If you make that commercial, you'll be competing with Coca-Cola."

I wanted to say, "Hey, Coca-Cola is paying *you*, not me." But I turned down the opportunity because of Michael's concern, and I appreciated the fact that he'd learned that loyalty, like integrity, is worth more than money.

chapter 10

In this chapter I offer more gifts that I wanted my children to be able to take with them when they left home.

INDEPENDENCE AND RESPONSIBILITY

We've talked about the long, hard process of loosening the grip and letting go. As we've seen, independence is something that comes gradually, over time. It's earned and learned through the practice of responsibility.

From the time they were old enough to follow simple instructions, our children were assigned regular household responsibilities. When they were preschoolers, that generally meant merely that they had to help pick up and put away their things. But as they grew older, they were expected to do their share of the regular household work. By the time they left home, all five of my children knew how to cook, wash clothes, clean house, and do their own ironing.

Because we felt that our children would benefit from more responsibility than we could give them at home, we encouraged them to find part-time jobs as teenagers. Ray and I were a little taken aback, though, when Ronnie took and passed a special road test to qualify as a school bus driver.

Driving a busload of students to and from school every day seemed like responsibility enough. Would he also be able to maintain discipline, given that many of the riders were his high school peers? "I think I can handle the job," he told us. And he did. He drove a regular bus route throughout his junior and senior years of high school.

On top of his ROTC schedule and his daily bus route, Ronnie got a part-time evening job at a Shoney's restaurant in Wilmington. He started as a dishwasher, progressed to cook, and continued working his way up the ranks. He came home one day to tell me he'd been promoted to manager. When I asked what the job entailed, he explained that he would be in charge of the entire evening shift—supervising the cooks and waitresses, overseeing the end-of-the-day cleanup of the kitchen and dining room, locking up the restaurant at midnight, and even making the night-drop of the cash register receipts at the bank.

While Ray and I felt extremely proud that the restaurant owner would place such trust in our high school son, we weren't sure we wanted him to take on that much responsibility. "You've got your bus route in the mornings and ROTC right after school. When are you going to do your schoolwork?" we wanted to know.

"I'll get it done at school or at home in the evening before I go in to work," he said. "I'll fit it in."

We finally gave him our tentative okay. "You can keep at it unless your grades begin to suffer," we told him. But they didn't. He managed the two jobs, ROTC, and school, enjoyed the independence that came from earning money of his own, and learned some major lessons about responsibility in the process.

None of our other children exhibited quite the drive Ronnie did, but they all gained some valuable work experience as teenagers. Delois worked as a part-time cashier at a local department store. Larry followed in his big brother's footsteps as a bus driver for our local school system his final year of high school and worked one summer before college at the Federal Paper plant. Roslyn worked for some time at a local McDonald's.

I worried that Michael wasn't getting the work experience his siblings had. In fairness to him, I have to say that sports absorbed a lot of his time after school, and much of each summer was taken up with baseball, Fellowship of Christian Athlete camps, and other special basketball camps he participated in. But he never seemed too anxious to find part-time work. In fact, when he had money, he was usually more than willing to work out a deal to pay Larry to haul in his share of firewood or to do some other household assignment so he could spend the time shooting baskets in the backyard.

The summer between his sophomore and junior years of high school, I was so determined for Michael to have a job that I approached one of my bank customers, a motel and restaurant owner, to ask if he might have some work—any work—for my teenage son. The man agreed to give Michael a job in his maintenance department; it was to be a temporary position—just for a couple weeks—until Michael had to leave for basketball camp.

The job didn't last even that long. Michael quit and walked three miles home when the employer could find nothing better for him to do than sweep off the sidewalk in front of the motel. Since the motel was located on one of the busiest streets in Wilmington, Michael worried that some of his friends might drive by and see him sweeping a sidewalk.

"Don't make me go back there," he pleaded, claiming that he wasn't really needed and that he wouldn't learn anything worthwhile in the few days he had left. While I felt bad that he wouldn't benefit from any more work experience that summer, I was glad he had gotten a small taste of the working world. It was certainly enough to help convince him of the value of pursuing a college education.

CONFIDENCE

Children develop confidence when their parents affirm them, show confidence in them, and support them. Children need to know that their parents think they're smart, good-looking, funny, kind, talented, and interesting. And kids may never realize those things are true unless we tell them or communicate in other ways.

I meet so many kids with no self-esteem. What they need more than anything else in the world is a mom or dad who will stand alongside them and say, "You can do it. I know you can." And if they fail, they need that same parent saying, "That's okay. I'm here. Everyone makes mistakes; everyone fails at something. Keep trying. If you want it bad enough, you can do it."

Whether your kids ever star in sports, or even play sports, they need parents on the sidelines of their lives cheering them on. You can always find something to cheer about. Whether your children win or lose, look for something they do well and praise them for that.

It's more important to cheer than to point out mistakes. Most kids know what they did wrong. They're usually hard enough on themselves. What they need most from parents is honest praise. That's what builds confidence.

Kids also gain self-confidence from success. As parents, we can help them achieve success by encouraging them to set realistic short-term goals. Each time they reach a goal, they gain confidence. Even the lessons learned in pursuit of an unattained goal often give them the confidence to try again.

This past year each of my five children took part in the program at our foundation's big annual fund-raising gala, held in one of Chicago's fanciest hotels. There, in the spotlight, on stage, in a ballroom filled with celebrities, high-powered business executives, and social leaders from Chicago and around the nation, Ronnie, Sis, Larry, and Roslyn all joined their brother Michael in making special presentations to some of our corporate sponsors.

Afterwards, a number of people commented to me on how poised and confident all my children seemed to be in front of an audience. "You must be very proud," they said.

And I was.

It reminded me of other people over the years who have observed Michael in a variety of settings—sitting and talking with a group of kids in a classroom, mixing with business tycoons, visiting with the family of a young cancer victim in a Ronald McDonald house, cutting up on the set during the making of a TV commercial—and have remarked on how comfortable and confident he has seemed in each situation.

I'm convinced that a big reason all of my children have grown into confident adults is that Ray and I were willing to expose our children to as many different experiences, people, and settings as possible when they were growing up. For example, when Larry and Michael played baseball for the Optimist Club, we were often the only black family that traveled with the team to tournaments around the state. Instead of seeing that as an intimidating situation, we viewed it as a positive opportunity for our sons to develop interracial friendships and gain experience they wouldn't otherwise have had. When the team played in the Shelby, North Carolina, area, the boys even got some exposure to the Native American culture of the kids they competed against.

But sports weren't the only source of varied experience for our kids. School clubs and activities gave them a variety of opportunities. We sent them to camps in the summer and took them on trips to visit relatives in places like Philadelphia and New York City. All this was in an attempt to expose the children to a variety of people and places.

I'm convinced that such experiences played a part in helping my adult children feel confident and at ease in whatever situation they find themselves in today. Those experiences also taught them to see people as people, apart from skin color, nationality, economic standing, or any other superficial characteristic—in other words, simply as human beings.

MORAL VALUES

Children, like most human beings, usually seek pleasure and avoid pain. It's up to us, as parents, to teach our children a higher standard; we must teach them to do what's right—despite the cost or the consequences, and no matter how hard it is.

A lot of parents these days are finding it pretty hard to teach their children right from wrong. It *is* hard without some basic standard of values. For me and my family, that standard was the Bible, the Ten Commandments, the Golden Rule.

Those things served not only as the foundation of, but also reinforcement for, what we tried to teach our kids. For example, when my children witnessed the disrespectful attitude one of their friends had for his or her parents, I'd pull out the

Ten Commandments and remind my children what the Bible says about needing to honor and respect one's parents. I wanted them to know that the values we taught in our family weren't just Jordan family rules. The things we said about honesty, respect, and so on weren't simply Ray's or my ideas; they reflected what the Bible said.

And that's why we taught those values.

SPIRITUAL FAITH

I'm usually a little sensitive about what I say on this subject, because I speak to a lot of groups made up of people with a lot of different backgrounds and beliefs. But my spiritual faith has been such a cornerstone of my own life and that of my family that I have to include it in any list of gifts I hope my children have received from me.

Church, like education, was one of those nonnegotiable priorities in the Jordan family. Regular weekly church attendance wasn't merely expected of our children; it was required.

There were times, of course—especially during the teenage years—when one of the kids would awaken on Sunday morning and protest that he just didn't feel up to going to church. I'd say, "If you feel that bad, I guess you won't feel good enough to go anywhere later or to play ball with friends this afternoon. You'll just have to stay in the house to rest and recover." Before long, the complainer would be showered and dressed for church.

Saturday night plans didn't alter my expectations at all. "It's fine if one of your buddies wants to sleep over tonight, as long as he's willing to go to church with us in the morning."

Human beings aren't just physical creatures; we're also social, emotional, intellectual, and spiritual beings. Just as we can't be healthy without exercising our physical bodies, we can't be healthy if we ignore any of those other areas. To be balanced, we have to work at developing and maintaining each aspect of our lives.

I've talked already about how church provided an important part of my support system as a parent and how the teachings of the church and the Bible reinforced the values I tried to teach my children.

But I've seen many other benefits, including some that people don't always realize can be attributed to spiritual faith. Just two quick examples.

I think spiritual faith can play a valuable role in how well we get along with and relate to other people — and not just in terms of the Golden Rule or putting other people first. For example, forgiveness is an important spiritual theme. When we understand that none of us is perfect, that we all need forgiveness from God, it makes it a lot easier to forgive others and be a more tolerant person.

I also think spiritual faith can help keep a person's feet on the ground. People often comment to me that there seems to be a real difference between Michael and a handful of big-talking, egotistical athletes who always seem to be saying to the world (with their attitude as well as their words), "Look at me: I'm the greatest."

And when people ask, "How is it that Michael, with all the ability he has and all the accolades he's received, can seem so humble?" I'd like to be able to take all the credit. But I can't.

Our family's spiritual faith and beliefs have a lot to do with it. I know my son well enough to realize he's very proud of the things he's worked so hard to achieve. He finds real satisfaction in knowing when he's done his best. But he, like all my other children, was taught that our Creator is the one who gives each of us special talents and abilities. Those things are gifts we need to be grateful for. And when we live each day with a sense of gratitude, that appreciation automatically tempers our pride. It helps us stay balanced. It helps keep even Air Jordan well grounded.

I really do believe that old saying, "The family that prays together stays together." There may be times when children stray from the spiritual teachings of their parents, but I also believe the Bible when it says, "Raise up a child in the way he should go, and when he is old he shall not depart from it" (Prov. 22:6). No matter where life takes our kids, if we try to teach and live out our spiritual faith in our homes, our children will be drawn back to their spiritual roots.

One of the primary ways Ray and I tried to instill spiritual faith in our children was through prayer. From the time they were old enough to say, "Now I lay me down to sleep," I said bedtime prayers with my children. They also took turns saying a blessing whenever we ate together. (We still take turns doing that.)

Prayer was always a crucial personal resource for me as a parent. When my babies cried and I didn't know what was wrong, I prayed for God to direct me, to help me know what to do. When my kids left for school in the morning, I prayed for their protection and safe return. When they struggled with a problem, I prayed and asked God to strengthen them. And when I'd done everything I could do in my own strength and power as a parent, I prayed simply, "Okay, Lord. You've got to take over from here."

There were countless times as a parent when I could depend only on God and prayer.

One of the things I do today to continue to foster my adult children's faith is to purchase for each a subscription to the monthly devotional guide *Daily Word*. While I can't ensure the guide's regular use, I do make a point of sometimes sharing a meditation from *Daily Word* when we get together as a family. And I was encouraged not long ago to learn that Ronnie had complained to Roslyn that his subscription had run out. When she told me about it, she added, "I went ahead and sent him a subscription myself."

The entire Jordan family has been through a lot of turmoil in recent years. Not just with Ray's sudden and senseless death and with the more recent loss of my only sister to cancer, but with a lot of other difficult changes—some very public and others very private. So much has happened that we don't understand. So many questions remain unanswered. But I can honestly say that it's faith that has gotten me and my family through. We've seen again and again what an important gift spiritual faith can be. We've learned that sometimes, on the darkest days, we can do nothing more than hold tight to that faith and trust God's grace to lead the way to another tomorrow.

At the UNICEF
award dinner in
1993. Audrey
Hepburn was
there too.

Parenthood. I think it's the toughest, most demanding, and sometimes most frustrating job in the world. It's a lifelong challenge that requires a lifetime commitment. And I'm convinced it's the most important and most rewarding experience we can have in this life.

But how do you know whether or not you've succeeded as a parent?

One night a few years ago I was sitting at home watching the evening news when *ABC News* anchor Peter Jennings began his "Person of the Week" feature. Suddenly Michael's face appeared on the screen: my youngest son was "Person of the Week"! Not the president of the United States. Not some international business leader. My son. And what made me proudest was Peter Jennings's statement that he was recognizing Michael not just for being the best basketball player in the world but because of "the kind of character he demonstrates off the court as well."

Those words warmed my heart as a mother, because I've always been more concerned about the kind of people my children are than what they achieve in their careers or how much money they make. On this score, all of my children do me proud, whether or not they ever get recognized for their virtues on network television.

This past summer our foundation provided a weekend workshop for parents and educators involved in the Michael Jordan Education Club, a nationwide pilot program we co-sponsored with the *Scholastic* Education Marketing Group. Roslyn helped coordinate the entire weekend and emceed part of the program. At the end of the final session, she closed the conference with a wonderfully meaningful prayer—for the people who participated, for the kids we all wanted to help, for a lasting impact of the conference, for journeying mercies, and for the great needs of our society.

I couldn't count the number of people who came up to me afterwards to express their appreciation for Roslyn's beautiful prayer. Their comments served to remind me that I'm prouder of the spiritually mature and sensitive person she has become than I am of all the academic honors she ever achieved.

During the time I was working on this book, in the fall of 1995, I learned that Michael had canceled an extensive promotional tour of Japan and the Far East at the very last minute. When I asked him why, Michael explained that the biggest reason was he'd decided he needed to spend more time with his three young children before the start of another long basketball season. Seeing him put the needs of his children ahead of business demands made me much prouder than another NBA scoring title would have.

At a recent family get-together, I overheard Larry and Delois, both of whom sell real estate part-time in addition to their various other business interests, talking about some of their personal sales strategies. Sis rattled off a list of creative marketing ideas. I could tell Larry was impressed when he said, "Some of those things could cost you a lot of money."

"I know," Sis admitted. "But I figure I've got to give each property my best shot, no matter how much it costs."

"You're right," Larry agreed. "If you're going to make it in real estate, you have to do the best you possibly can for each client."

Here were two of my children agreeing on and holding each other accountable to the highest standard of excellence. They both took it for granted that "you have to do the best you possibly can." Just hearing them affirm that made me feel more proud than any business success they could possibly achieve.

I also see the strong leadership role Ronnie (like his brothers) has assumed in our family since Ray's death. It's evidence of the same strength of character that enables him as a first sergeant to successfully command 130 Army personnel in his computer training unit at Fort Bragg. And it makes me prouder than all the awards and medals he's received during his twenty-plus years in the service.

The character I see in all my children makes me proud to be their mother. It makes all the effort, all the years, and all the tears seem worthwhile. It makes me think Ray and I must have done something right.

How do you know whether or not you've succeeded as a parent?

Ronnie talks to me about one of his recent visits to the doctor's office with his daughters. Sis phones to report on the latest accomplishments of her teenagers. I see Larry and his family taking special trips together. Michael laughs as he tells me how his boys want Daddy to drive them to school every morning he's home. Ros and I talk nearly every day, because she's active in the work of our foundation and always wants to know how her mother is doing.

When I see and experience the commitment each of my children makes to family, that also makes me proud. They choose to make family a priority. They too put family first.

As a parent, that's my greatest reward.

ACKNOWLEDGMENTS

I planned to write this book before Ray's death because so many people have approached us over the years to say what a wonderful family we have. I want to thanks all those folks for their inspiration and the motivation they gave me to write this book. One of the reasons I completed this project was to encourage them in return. I wanted other parents to find strength and hope in hearing that parenting is never an easy job. It takes commitment, dedication, and a lot of hard work. I only share my experience here in the hope that it will inspire others to know they are not alone in their parenting struggles.

To the people who played the biggest direct role in the completion and publication of this book, I'd also like to express my gratitude. Thanks, Gregg, for your ability to draw out and capture my thoughts and feelings in such an effective way; you helped me walk back through my life to those times and places when I vowed to put family first. Thank you to our editor, Barbara Moulton, who was always such a positive, encouraging, joy to work with. Thank you to Harper Collins San Francisco for being willing to let me write the book I wanted to write. And appreciation also to Charice White for helping organize some of my initial thoughts and to Cynthia Patrick who helped me with computer input.

I also have to acknowledge God's help—in putting together this book and throughout my life. I thank him everyday for the blessings he bestowed on me and my family, for the strength he has provided me to carry on then and now. Even in my lowest points, especially at those times, he has been there with me to offer hope.

I also owe much to my own parents for the love and guidance they gave me and for the values they handed down to me, values Ray I wanted to instill in our children. To my only sister, Ruth, whose valued leadership, guidance, and love I lost to cancer just eight months after Ray's death. And to my loving brother Edward Peoples, Jr., whose love and support helped restore my hope when I wasn't sure where I was going.

In addition I need to acknowledge three other people who were important resources in my parenting. My mother-in-law, Ms. Bell Jordan, became a dear friend as she helped me learn about motherhood. And Dr. and Mrs. Sutton, who never closed their door when I needed help and advice about one of my children.

Finally, the people I'd like to thank most of all are my children and their families. Their love has always been my greatest inspiration as a parent. And their encouragement to write about my parenting has been my biggest inspiration in writing this book about the Jordan family experience.

Thank you to Ronnie for always giving me back so much love. And to his wife, Blanca, and their daughters, Nickie and Jamie (who was named after Ray) for the joy they bring to my life.

Thank you to Delois who is free-hearted and generous with most anything she has, including her love for me. She worked hard to find her own space and place in the family, and now her children Cory and Sherri (whom I'm proud to claim as my oldest grandchildren) demand the same.

Thank you to Larry. You have to know his way to see the easy, quiet manner in which he shows his love and affection—always sincere and committed. To Angela, who has become like a daughter to me, and who has given me the thrill of watching two more precious grandchildren, Alexis and Justin, begin to grow up.

Thank you to Michael, who always has a way of making himself and his love known—who himself loves the attention and affection of the family. And to Juanita, his wife, who is working so hard and learning so much about motherhood from my grandchildren Jeffrey, Marcus, and Jasmine.

And thank you to Roslyn who gives love to us all with her written notes, her poems, and her prayers. Daily she reminds us of our blessings and our Savior as she reaches out to help me, her brothers and sister, and her nieces and nephews in any way she can.

To all my children and grandchildren I say thank you for the love and joy you have given me. As your families continue to grow, I hope you will always work hard with them so that your children may have the values Ray and I worked so hard to give you.

Love always, Mom.